1/2012

Paint Your Career Green

Get a Green Job Without Starting Over

JIST
Works
America's Career Publisher®

Stan Schatt and
Michele Lobl

PAINT YOUR CAREER GREEN

© 2012 by Stan Schatt and Michele Lobl

7321 Shadeland Station, Suite 200
Indianapolis, IN 46256-3923
Phone: 800-648-JIST   Fax: 877-454-7839
E-mail: info@jist.com   Website: www.jist.com

Visit our website at **www.jist.com.** Find out about our products, get free tables of contents and sample pages, order a catalog, and link to other career-related sites.

Quantity discounts are available for JIST books. Please call 800-648-JIST or visit www.jist.com for a free catalog and more information.

Development Editor: Dave Anderson
Cover Designer: Alan Evans
Page Layout: Aleata Halbig
Proofreaders: Paula Lowell, Jeanne Clark
Indexer: Cheryl Lenser

Printed in the United States of America

16 15 14 13 12 11   9 8 7 6 5 4 3 2 1

Library of Congress Cataloging-in-Publication Data

Schatt, Stanley.
  Paint your career green : get a green job without starting over / Stan
Schatt and Michele Lobl.
      p. cm.
  Includes bibliographical references and index.
  ISBN 978-1-59357-859-6 (alk. paper)
  1. Environmental sciences--Vocational guidance. 2. Career changes. 3.
Job hunting. 4. Vocational guidance. I. Lobl, Michele, 1945- II.
Title.
  GE60.S33 2011
  333.72023--dc23
                                        2011020497

We have been careful to provide accurate information in this book, but it is possible that errors and omissions have been introduced. Please consider this in making any career plans or other important decisions. Trust your own judgment above all else and in all things.

Trademarks: All brand names and product names used in this book are trade names, service marks, trademarks, or registered trademarks of their respective owners.

ISBN 978-1-59357-859-6

This book is dedicated to my husband, Tom, who encouraged me to consolidate my years of "job skills" training into a book, and to my co-author, Stan, who said "let's write a book together." I would also like to recognize my mother, Evelyn, who has always stood behind me and encouraged and praised me for all accomplishments. She has been a "role model" throughout my life.

Thanks,

Michele

I'd like to dedicate this book to my wife, Jane. One wonderful thing about being married 45 years is that I know she will be the first person I see every morning and the last person I see every night. She completes me.

Stan

TABLE OF CONTENTS

The Current Job Environment: A Reality Check

At the time we're writing this book, the unemployment rate is hovering around 10 percent. In fact, the real unemployment rate is much higher because many people have stopped looking for a job and therefore are no longer counted as "unemployed."

There is good news, however. This might be the best time ever to paint your career green by moving into an environmentally friendly role. As we'll show in this book, the future is likely to see an explosion in the number of "green jobs," with corresponding new career tracks. Later, we'll explain the distinction between jobs and careers, but first let us explain why this trend toward green jobs is so exciting—and why it will change forever some of the basic tenets most of us have come to believe.

First, we need to understand the underlying problems that are driving unemployment even as green jobs and green careers gain momentum. It doesn't take a genius to recognize the obstacles people face when it comes to securing a job:

- *The World Is Flat.* Columnist Thomas Friedman wrote this very provocative book in which he pointed to the fact that the world has gotten a lot more interconnected when it comes to commerce. People joke about the likelihood that their next customer support call to a credit card vendor or a PC manufacturer will be answered by someone working in India. In fact, outsourcing is not limited to customer support. It has expanded to many other areas, including accounting, computer-aided drawing, and research of all kinds. These jobs will never come back to the United States because companies have become accustomed to the low pay scales abroad. We'll see shortly that one major advantage of green jobs is that they remain local and cannot be outsourced.

- **Companies are encouraged to outsource.** To compound matters, lobbyists have convinced congress to write favorable tax laws that actually make it *beneficial* for companies to move their offices overseas. Manufacturing was once a bedrock for the middle class. The reality is that the manufacturing jobs that have left the U.S. will never return. The landscape is littered with empty factories that once paid very good salaries for work that did not require a college education. Thankfully, green products will shift the manufacturing emphasis from low-wage jobs to a highly educated workforce.

- **Oil dependence is a security risk.** The U.S. currently imports around 60 percent of the oil it consumes, and the price per barrel continues to rise. Government officials also point to the security danger of relying on unstable governments in the Middle East as well as third-world countries for the lifeblood to run our factories and homes. Each additional dollar we spend to import a diminishing resource like oil is, in effect, a tax on businesses and on their customers. Consumers react to increasing gasoline costs by cutting back on their spending. These cuts in spending hit businesses' bottom lines. As their profits decline, these companies reduce their overhead by cutting employees. In contrast, green energy initiatives will eliminate this energy tax and fatten corporate bottom lines enough to permit additional hiring.

In short, some of the issues that have created the recent downturn in employment are driving—and will continue to drive—the move toward a greener workforce.

What *Is* a Green Job?

We've mentioned green jobs but have not really defined what the term means. Green jobs are those jobs that maintain, preserve, and restore the environment while providing a livable wage. Recently the U.S. Department of Labor's Bureau of Labor Statistics (BLS) proposed a definition of green jobs as those jobs "related to preserving or restoring the environment." The Bureau of Labor Statistics lists seven economic activities under which green jobs fall:

- Renewable energy
- Energy efficiency
- Greenhouse gas reduction

- Pollution reduction and cleanup
- Recycling and waste reduction
- Agricultural and natural resources conservation
- Education, compliance, public awareness, and training

These economic activities result in the production of green goods and services that fall into four types:

- Direct green goods and services (including weatherization of buildings)
- Indirect green goods and services (for example, goods containing recycled materials)
- Specialized inputs (for example, wind-turbine blades and mass-transit rail cars)
- Distribution of green goods that fall into one of the first three categories

Some refer to green jobs as "green-collar" jobs. Green-collar jobs are traditional blue-collar jobs that have been converted to green jobs because they now are based on sustainable resources. Many experts believe that traditional blue-collar manufacturing jobs are lost forever, in part because it is so much cheaper to outsource these jobs to countries with far lower wages. Green-collar jobs, however, require state-of-the-art technology and well-educated workers. President Obama and others are hopeful that this country can capture a large share of such jobs in the future. Other characteristics of green-collar jobs are that they will offer career tracks in vocational and trade areas associated with eco-friendly industries and will pay a livable wage sufficient to support a family.

The Pressure on Companies to Paint Themselves Green

Not too long ago, one of us (Stan) published a report that rated major companies on how green they were. The reaction was surprising. Many companies that did not score well responded by lobbying for a higher score. The companies that *did* score well wanted permission to use quotes from the report to generate positive publicity. Fortune 500 companies are *very* concerned about how the public perceives their efforts to reduce their carbon footprint.

Companies such as Hewlett-Packard, Dell, and Cisco document their efforts to reduce their carbon footprints in great detail on their websites. Most large companies now have highly salaried employees charged with directing their green initiatives. They keep detailed records on such things as how much their companies have reduced their air travel by holding video conferences, how successful they have been in eliminating plastic water bottles, and how much they have increased their use of renewable energy resources.

For example, under a section on its website entitled "Environmental Responsibility," Dell's comments include the following:

> When selecting substances used to design our products, we are guided by a precautionary approach. This means eliminating environmentally sensitive substances from our products wherever cost-effective, safer alternatives are available....

> We are also taking steps to minimize the environmental impacts of our manufacturing operations. In September 2007, we became the first major computer company to go carbon neutral. Late in fiscal year 2008, Dell increased the amount of green power purchased from utility providers to 81,000 megawatt-hours (MWh) per year, which represents enough power to serve Dell's entire headquarters campus in Round Rock, Texas, in fiscal year 2009.

The reason companies such as Dell are so anxious to describe their environmental efforts is that more and more customers and stockholders are demanding eco-friendly policies. No company wants to give a competitor an edge, so there is spirited competition for companies to show they are leaders when it comes to environmental concerns.

These companies are not limited to the IT industry. Each year *Corporate Knights,* a magazine focused on "green capitalism," publishes a list of the top 100 most sustainable corporations. General Electric was the winner in 2010. As companies ramp up their sustainability efforts, they create more and more positions for employees to audit and analyze energy use, write reports on environmental efforts and compliance, and publicize results. If and when carbon credit trading becomes a reality, these same companies will be hiring people to manage their carbon credits as part of their overall sustainability efforts, which could mean more opportunities for you.

Government Legislation and Green Industries

The 2009 American Recovery and Reinvestment Act (ARRA) earmarked $500 million for green jobs training. In addition, President Obama's 2011 fiscal budget included $85 million for the creation of green jobs. These allocations, though, are just a drop in the bucket compared to the money in the ARRA targeting the development of new green technology. Among the areas targeted were the following:

- $17.7 billion for public-transportation initiatives
- $3.2 billion for energy efficiency and conservation
- $4.5 billion for smart-grid projects
- $700 million for the development of alternative-energy vehicles
- $3.69 billion for DOD energy-efficiency projects
- $1.2 billion for water-related projects
- $300 million to reduce diesel emissions
- $884 million for energy-efficient retrofits to older buildings
- $2 billion for the development of advanced battery systems

The fact that so much of the stimulus bill was focused on green energy solutions shows that there is growing recognition that this country's future depends on how quickly we can move toward creating a robust sustainable-energy infrastructure.

These funds will spawn the development of thriving new green industries—new businesses that will design, build, and sell alternative-energy vehicles, and research, manufacture, and install smart grids and other environmentally friendly technologies. The trend is clear: As products move from the research and design stages to production and distribution phases, there will be increased need for people trained and ready to fill new career positions. Fuel-cell batteries will need to be produced, distributed, sold, and then repaired. Old diesel engines will need to be retrofitted. New public-transportation initiatives will require people to plan, schedule, analyze, and drive new vehicles.

All this money pumped into previously money-starved green industries will ultimately result in a seismic change in this country's infrastructure, but it will take a couple of years for this massive influx of cash to wind its way through the system and start to show results in the form of new jobs. When it does, the job titles may be completely new. In the meantime, it's a perfect time to prepare for this new world and be ready to move into a promising green career track when the opportunity arises. This book will help you do just that.

It Can Be Easy Turning Green

Green technology can sound exotic, especially if you have been in a traditional manufacturing job such as working at an auto plant. You might ask yourself what someone who has been a fleet sales manager for an automotive company would know about green technology. The answer might be very little, but that person already has experience with fleet sales, and it's not that difficult for him to earn credentials to paint his career green and manage electric or hybrid car sales. Similarly, people who have been technical trainers or teachers and have years of valuable experience can credential themselves using the approach we suggest in Chapter 10 and easily become solar, wind, or geothermal technical trainers.

In fact, many green energy industry positions look and feel very much like similar jobs in other industries *except* for a veneer of green expertise. The following table shows examples of how it's possible to leverage previous experience in such jobs to move into a green career field.

HOW TRADITIONAL CAREERS CAN BE TINTED GREEN		
Old Title	**New Title**	**Green Knowledge Tint**
Trainer	Green Sustainability Trainer	Knowledge of green sustainability issues
Accountant	Eco-Accountant	Knowledge of green technology costs
Financial Analyst	Energy Auditor	Knowledge of energy costs
Construction Sales Manager	Solar Energy Sales Manager	Knowledge of solar technology
Machinist	Wind Turbine Fabricator	Knowledge of wind technology
Lab Technician	Hazardous Materials Specialist	40 hours of training on hazardous materials

Old Title	New Title	Green Knowledge Tint
Travel Agent	Eco-Travel Agent	Knowledge of sustainable energy practices and green venues
Civil Engineer	Transportation Environmental Planner	Transportation Professional Certificate from the Institute of Transportation Engineers

Painter's Tip: You need to paint yourself with enough of a green credential to make the first cut. Only then can you leverage your previous work experience.

It's Time for a Change

The fact that you are reading this book means that you already have taken the first step toward painting your career green. In many ways, now is the ideal time to make a change. Because green industries are in their infancy, even minimal training will give you an edge and make you a valuable asset. When green industries begin to mature several years from now, educational requirements are bound to be become far more demanding as new types of green certification become standard.

As we have indicated, federal funds are creating brand-new types of green occupations. Equally important, a significant number of existing occupations are in the process of being given a green tinge. If you already are an accountant or a travel agent, becoming a green accountant or a green travel agent will set you apart from the competition and position you for rapid growth in the future.

As a green pioneer, you'll be in a position similar to people who joined the computer industry when it was in its infancy, well before there was a formal computer science major available in college. It's an exciting time. By the time you work your way through this book, you'll be well on your way down a career path that should provide you with far greater opportunities than your present occupation. Equally important, you'll be helping to build a cleaner, greener world for the next generation.

CHAPTER 1

The World Is Turning Green— Careers with a Future

Sometimes it's difficult to recognize the revolution taking place around you because each change seems so small. Like when you read the morning newspaper and see an advertisement for a new car that plugs into the electric outlet in your garage. Or when you talk with friends who are remodeling and say they are considering solar panels. The move toward energy efficiency and a cleaner environment is accelerating, and that trend is likely to result in a vast number of jobs across many industries. One question you might be thinking is, "Where will these jobs be found?"

This chapter will answer that question. You'll learn how several industries you might never have thought twice about are growing and creating brand-new, well-paying jobs that can't be outsourced. This chapter takes a closer look at a number of green career areas worth exploring. If you find an area of interest, see Chapter 10 to find out where to learn more about educational programs to help you acquire the necessary knowledge to help you make the transition.

Energy

The American Solar Energy Society commissioned a report by Management Information Services Inc. revealing that as many as 37 million jobs can be generated by the renewable energy and energy efficiency industries in the U.S. by 2030—more than 17 percent of all anticipated U.S. employment. There are exciting developments in several different areas of renewable energy, though the U.S. has barely touched the surface when it comes to generating jobs from this area. (By contrast, Germany has around a quarter of the U.S. population but generates four times the number of voltaic solar jobs and five times the number of jobs associated with wind energy.) Let's take a look at some of the areas with the greatest potential.

Solar Energy

Of all the sustainable energy options, solar has progressed the furthest. The rise in electricity rates as a result of continuing increases in the cost of oil have made solar power more attractive. That's particularly true because of federal programs such as the federal solar investment tax credit (ITC) as well as various incentive programs in a number of states. These programs have made it more financially advantageous to install solar equipment, precipitating an 18 percent increase in solar installations in 2009 over 2008. *Solarbuzz* reported that the U.S. solar energy revenue grew 36 percent in 2009 and forecast that the industry would enjoy a tenfold increase by 2014.

More than 850 American companies are currently involved in manufacturing, installing, and selling solar system components. That number is bound to increase over the next several years. In 2009, the U.S. solar industry supported 17,000 new jobs. Total employment in the U.S. solar industry at the end of 2009 was 46,000. That number was expected to exceed 60,000 in 2010.

One reason there is such a bright future for solar power is that several solar technologies have emerged from research labs and now are commercially available. The cost of very promising photovoltaic (PV) technology is declining rapidly. Photovoltaic chips reside between solar panels and help turn sunlight into electricity. PV deployments were up 40 percent in 2009 compared to 2008. In the United States, more than 34,000 PV installations were completed in 2009.

At the same time, Concentrating Solar Power (CSP) technologies leverage mirrors to heat hydrogen and power-generator pistons that produce electricity. Four new CSP plants were built in 2009 in Arizona, California, and Hawaii, and plans are underway to build several additional plants by 2011. One very special attribute of CSP systems is thermal storage. This means that systems can generate electricity whenever it's needed and not just when the sun is shining. That ability makes this technology attractive to utility companies.

A third solar technology, low-temperature thermal, is finding a market in the form of solar water heaters and pool heaters. Interestingly enough, around a quarter of all water heaters installed in Hawaii are solar. Federal stimulus dollars have been specifically earmarked for replacing conventional water heaters with solar water heaters.

Careers in solar energy can take a variety of different forms, and solar companies have some unique job titles. Table 1.1 lists a few of these jobs. In Chapter 10, you'll find a detailed list of training opportunities to prepare you for these specific, fast-growing occupations.

TABLE 1.1: REPRESENTATIVE SOLAR INDUSTRY JOB TITLES

Solar Engineer	Solar PV Installer
Solar Field Engineer	Solar Sales Representative
Solar Installation Manager	Solar Site Assessor
Solar Power Designer	Solar Site Auditor
Solar Power Electrical Engineer	Solar System Estimator
Solar Project Foreman	

Remember, you don't need to become the world's foremost expert on the subject of solar energy to get a job in this sector. One major solar company recently advertised for a regional sales manager position. The company wanted all the requisite skills that any company would want for such a position: sales management experience, channel development experience, and so on. Finally, the ad stated that "The ideal candidate brings an enthusiasm for saving the environment through our philosophy of sustainability—'clean energy from sand and sun.'" That was the extent of the green credential required for the job. Sometimes you only need to convince a hiring manager that you have the right attitude and enough knowledge of green technology to complement all of your work experience from your previous career.

Wind Power

Just as with solar energy, there is a good deal of excitement over the growth of wind power. The Union of Concerned Scientists found that wind creates 2.4 times more jobs than coal or natural gas during plant construction and 1.5 times more jobs during long-term operations and maintenance. Wind currently supplies around 2 percent of the world's energy needs. At this point, the U.S. is trailing China when it comes to wind power development.

Still, 2009 was a record year for wind power development in the U.S., with more than 10,000 MegaWatts (MW) in new installations. Wind power has been growing at more than 25 percent each year in the U.S. It is estimated that there is enough wind capacity within the United States to provide nine times the total energy consumed in 2009. The U.S. wind power industry started 2010 with around 85,000 jobs distributed across all 50 states, a number that will continue to rise.

Table 1.2 provides a representative list of typical job titles associated with the wind energy industry. The American Wind Energy Association website (www.careersinwind.com) includes a jobs board for both job seekers and employers. Some jobs require a two-year technical degree or at least a certificate. A significant percentage of jobs at wind plants are for turbine assemblers and turbine maintenance workers. Many of the specialized wind-power training programs are described in Chapter 10.

TABLE 1.2: REPRESENTATIVE WIND ENERGY JOB TITLES

Community Wind Development Specialist	Turbine Software Developer
Director of Erection and Commissioning	Turbine Wiring Site Specialist
Electrical Engineer—Wind	Wind Energy Sales Representative
Health and Safety Manager	Wind Facility Manager
Mechanical Engineer—Wind	Wind Turbine Electrician
Meteorologist	Wind Turbine Installer
Procurement Specialist	Wind Turbine Technician

Some positions, especially the engineering and scientific jobs, require four-year college degrees. Note, though, that certificate programs are perfect ways for engineers to move smoothly into a green-related career without starting over. Similarly, computer programmers worried about the out-sourcing of so many software development jobs can quickly learn how to program turbines and move smoothly into a career path that is likely never to be shipped overseas.

Finally, there are many jobs in the rapidly growing wind power industry with the same job titles in other industries. Technical writers can paint themselves green enough to be able to write about wind power. The same principle holds true for trainers, salespeople, factory supervisors, and facility managers. Besides the need for assemblers and factory workers of all kinds, the wind power industry requires truck drivers to move the massive turbines, marketing professionals to market this energy product, and new business developers to convince utility companies to embrace this technology. Whatever your background, wind can carry you to a new career.

While some types of wind power jobs—such as those in scientific research—can be found anywhere in the country, certain states dominate when it comes to wind capacity. The American Wind Energy Association listed the following five states as the leaders in wind power installations as of the end of 2009:

1. Texas

2. Iowa

3. California

4. Washington

5. Oregon

Several other states have enormous wind capacity, namely Colorado, Kansas, Minnesota, Nebraska, New Mexico, North Dakota, Oklahoma, South Dakota, and Wyoming. So if you're living in one of these states, you might want to prepare yourself now because they are poised for rapid growth.

Keep in mind that the specific knowledge you need for the majority of wind power–related jobs can be obtained in a year or less. Iowa Lakes Community College, for example, has a terrific two-year degree program in Wind Energy and Turbine Technology, but it's possible to obtain a certificate after only three semesters.

Geothermal Energy

The water and steam below our feet is another source of renewable energy. A series of pipes can bring heated water to a home heat pump that converts the energy into a form that can warm a home. At this time, other countries such as Japan and Canada have made far more use of this form of energy than we have in the U.S. At the moment, geothermal provides for only around 1 percent of our energy needs.

That figure is expected to grow, however. A new report by the Geothermal Energy Association (GEA) shows that there has been strong growth in new geothermal power projects in the United States continuing into 2010. New geothermal projects increased by 26 percent in 2009. The report identifies a total of 188 projects under development in a number of states, including Alaska, Arizona, California, Colorado, Florida, Hawaii, Idaho, Nevada, New Mexico, Oregon, Utah, and Washington. In the 2010 report, Nevada continued to be the leading state for new geothermal energy. However, the fastest-growing geothermal power states were Utah (which quadrupled its geothermal power under development), New Mexico (which tripled), Idaho (which doubled), and Oregon (which reported a 50 percent increase). The Geothermal Association's website makes it possible for you to click on a state and actually see what geothermal projects are underway there (http://geo-energy.org/plants_dev.aspx).

In addition, the U.S. government added new federal tax grant provisions in the 2009 stimulus bill. The GEA report pointed to more than $600 million in research into new technology that will result in "135 projects in 25 states over the next two years. Stimulus funds are earmarked to support development of enhanced geothermal systems technology, new drilling and exploration techniques, as well as geothermal power production from oil and gas wells."

In 2008, the Geothermal Energy Association estimated there were around 25,000 jobs associated with the geothermal industry. Yet the Western Governors' Association has estimated the *potential* jobs in the geothermal industry at 100,000. These jobs include welders; mechanics; pipefitters; plumbers; machinists; electricians; carpenters; construction and drilling equipment operators and excavators; surveyors; architects and designers; geologists; hydrologists; electrical, mechanical, and structural engineers; HVAC technicians; food processing specialists; aquaculture and horticulture specialists; resort managers; spa developers; researchers; and government employees.

Although Chapter 10 provides a detailed list of training opportunities to help you prepare for a job in the geothermal industry, it's also possible to educate yourself at home. The HeatSpring Learning Institute in Massachusetts offers a six-week video-based distance-learning program. If you pass the test at the end, you earn an entry-level Geothermal Professional certificate. There are also courses offered in partnership with the International Ground Source Heat Pump Association (IGSHPA) at a variety of locations.

If you pass the open-book exam, you earn an IGSHPA certificate as an accredited geothermal installer.

Table 1.3 describes some typical geothermal energy job titles. In addition, a quick look at the Jobs in Geothermal website (http://jobsingeothermal.jobamatic.com/a/jobs/find-jobs) reveals a number of employers seeking qualified individuals.

TABLE 1.3: REPRESENTATIVE GEOTHERMAL INDUSTRY JOB TITLES

Director of Compliance	Geothermal Systems Engineer
Geophysicist	HVAC Service Technician
Geothermal Analyst	Market Development Manager, Geothermal
Geothermal Driller	
Geothermal Engineer	Resource Manager, Geothermal
Geothermal Project Manager	

Bioenergy

People have used organic mass for fuel for ages, whether we're talking about the pioneers who burned wood to keep warm or people today who drive cars fueled by ethanol made from corn. Of course ethanol has its detractors because it takes a good deal of cost and energy to produce this fuel. There are many other organic mass candidates to replace or supplement ethanol (corn) including switchgrass, algae, and clean municipal wastes. Other countries have turned to other types of organic mass to create bioenergy as well. Brazil, for example, has become largely fuel self-reliant by transforming sugarcane into bioenergy. The Energy Independence and Security Act of 2007 requires that renewable fuels supply at least 36 billion gallons of U.S. motor fuels by 2022. In 2008, this country produced around 9 billion gallons of ethanol.

The Department of Energy reports that more than 400,000 jobs were tied to the ethanol industry in 2009. Bio Economic Research Associates has forecast that if the bioenergy industry expands beyond ethanol and meets current mandates, between one and two million jobs could be added in the next 15 to 20 years.

When it comes to producing bioenergy, the supply chain has a variety of different parts. This chain includes the farmers, biochemists, engineers, and scientists who are responsible for producing the feedstocks to be converted into energy. It also includes technicians and engineers as well as microbiologists and plant operators tied to biorefineries. Finally there are all the people responsible for transporting the biofuels, including truck drivers, pipeline operators, barge operators, railcar operators, and train station operators.

Not only can foodstuffs, plants, and trees be converted into energy, but it's also possible to convert waste into energy. Trash is first stripped of any recyclables and then heated in a furnace. The heat is used to turn water into steam that in turn drives large turbines that generate electricity. That means that all of our landfills are potential sources of energy and, equally important, a potential source of jobs.

In 2010, Florida passed a law that promotes recycling and provides a major opportunity for waste-to-energy to grow as an industry. The law specifies a goal of recycling recyclable solid waste by 75 percent by the year 2020. The state is promoting the production of renewable energy from solid waste; each megawatt-hour produced by a waste-to-energy facility counts as one ton of recycled material and is applied toward meeting the recycling goals.

As of 2010, there were 89 waste-to-energy plants in the U.S. and 400 plants in Europe. Waste-to-energy requires a variety of different workers, including engineers, analysts, administrators and managers, technicians, and so on. Table 1.4 provides some typical waste-to-energy job titles. This list was taken from an actual job board sponsored by the Solid Waste Association of North America (SWANA). More information on this group, including additional job listings and resources, can be found on its website: www.swana.org.

TABLE 1.4: REPRESENTATIVE WASTE-TO-ENERGY JOB TITLES

Civil/Environmental Permitting Engineer	Renewable Energy Project Manager
Director of Environmental Services	Solid Waste Administrator
Facility Technician	Solid Waste General Services Superintendent
Landfill Manager	

Hydroelectric Power

We usually associate hydroelectric power with large-scale dams. In fact, we generate enough hydroelectric power in this country to supply the electricity needs of 28 million households. Around 90 percent of all renewable energy in this country comes from hydroelectric sources.

A 2010 report sponsored by the National Hydropower Association estimates that there are between 200,000 and 300,000 jobs currently associated with the hydroelectricity industry. Strong government support could boost that number to 1.4 million by 2025. The report identified job growth opportunities in Washington state, Oregon, California, and Arkansas tied to water resources; manufacturing states including Pennsylvania, Wisconsin, Tennessee, and Ohio; and states with advanced hydroelectric potential including Tennessee, Maine, New York, and Florida.

Because building huge dams is expensive, there is a growing movement toward building small-scale hydroelectric plants. The National Hydropower Association has been lobbying Congress to provide financial incentives for this new technology. These smaller plants would add to future job opportunities in this field.

The hydropower industry employs a variety of different professionals, including hydrologists, hydraulic engineers, and technicians. Although professions such as hydrologists and engineers require four-year college degrees, a number of positions such as hydroelectric plant efficiency operator only require some technical training. Table 1.5 provides a sampling of hydropower job titles.

TABLE 1.5: REPRESENTATIVE HYDROPOWER JOB TITLES

Civil Engineer—Hydraulic	Hydroelectric Plant Efficiency Operator
Electrician—Power Systems	
Geologist	Hydroelectric Plant Installation Technician
Hydroelectric Equipment Operator	Hydroelectric Plant Mechanic
Hydroelectric Operations Maintenance Worker	Hydrologist
	Micro Hydropower System Installer

Hydrogen Fuel Cells

Hydrogen is our most common element, and hydrogen fuel cells can be used to power anything from a handheld device to a bus. What is particularly appealing about hydrogen power is that it is perfectly clean energy that is pollution free, yet it is so abundant that it does not require us to import it. Even better, hydrogen power is twice as efficient as traditional combustion technology, according to the U.S. Department of Energy.

But the power of hydrogen is difficult to harness. The version of hydrogen power clearly in the lead right now is the Polymer Electrolyte Membrane (PEM) fuel cell. Explaining how this technology is beyond the scope of this book; however, the Department of Energy has a webpage devoted to hydrogen power that goes into great detail on this technology (www1.eere. energy.gov/hydrogenandfuelcells/pdfs/doe_h2_fuelcell_factsheet.pdf).

Right now hydrogen fuel cells are still too expensive and lack the durability necessary to become a major source of power in this country. The Department of Energy has a number of research projects underway to overcome these problems. Automobile companies are doing their own research and planning models for the near future that will run on hydrogen fuel cells. The Department of Energy has a website devoted to career opportunities in hydrogen power that includes jobs as well as lists of employers who are active in the hydrogen power industry (www.fuelcells.org/ced/employ.html).

A number of colleges and universities offer training in hydrogen power, and these programs are listed in Chapter 10. One of the most innovative programs is Hocking College's two-year program in Alternative Energy and Fuel Cells. Hocking's program trains students in non-fossil fuel energy applications. The course of study includes mobile, stationary, and portable fuel cells as well as solar and wind power as energy sources. Table 1.6 provides titles for some typical hydrogen power jobs currently being advertised. Although a number of positions in this field require extensive education at a four-year university, there will be an increasing number of very well-paying green-collar positions at the technician level that people can train for by taking courses in shorter specialized programs such as those offered by Hocking College.

TABLE 1.6: REPRESENTATIVE HYDROGEN POWER JOB TITLES

Advanced Battery Development Technician	Mechanical Engineer
Corrosion Technician	Proton Exchange FC Membrane Technician
Cryogenics Technician	Solid Oxide FC Production Technician
Fuel Cells Application Engineer	
Hydrogen Storage Technician	Vehicular Laboratory Technician
Manufacturing Equipment Engineer	

Smart Grids

Right now this country has a complex infrastructure designed to take energy generated by fossil fuels and transmit it to where it's needed. Although it makes sense for our current energy grid to focus on areas of the country where fossil fuels are processed, those are not necessarily where the next generation of energy resources will come from.

Take Nebraska, for example. Although Nebraska is not thought of as a major source of oil, it's an excellent place for large wind turbines. It's one thing to create energy using sustainable resources like solar, geothermal, and wind power. It's quite another to transmit this energy from where it is created to factories and homes where it is needed. That's why there's such a need for a smart grid. Theoretically, a smart grid gathers information all along its path and allows automated control that can respond to changing energy needs.

Smart grids will be able to respond to consumer demand as well as utility company priorities by managing power requirements in both directions. They will be able to provide consumers with accurate information on usage and offer lower rates for energy not consumed during peak hours. Another key component will be the ability to store energy created from sources such as solar and wind power so that they can be used when needed. Smart grids would be able to integrate all clean energy technologies including electric cars, rooftop systems, wind farms, and geothermal power generation.

Title XIII of the Energy Independence and Security Act of 2007 (EISA) sets goals for modernizing the nation's electricity transmission and distribution system through a smart grid and authorizes funding for smart grid development and demonstration projects and matching funds for smart grid investments. The Stimulus Bill in 2009 appropriated $4.5 billion for Title XIII projects and other efforts to modernize the grid.

The creation of a smart grid is already creating a demand for jobs. KEMA, one of the leading energy consulting companies, estimates that 280,000 jobs will result from creating a smart grid. Equally important, these consultants estimate that 140,000 of these jobs will be ongoing after the grid is built. These jobs create opportunities for people who already have job experience in areas such as software development, security, project management, procurement, new business creation, and sales, after they have painted themselves green enough to show that they understand the nature of smart grid technology. Table 1.7 provides a list of some representative smart grid jobs.

TABLE 1.7: REPRESENTATIVE SMART GRID JOB TITLES

Smart Grid Engineer	Smart Grid Security Manager
Smart Grid Consultant	Commercial Manager—Smart Grid Proposals
Smart Grid Solutions Business Development Specialist	Smart Grid Engagement Manager
Smart Grid Integration Architect	Smart Grid Equipment Manager

Water Quality

There is very little drinkable water on this planet, and the situation could get far worse in the future. Preserving and expanding the amount of drinkable water and improving water quality is a high-growth area when it comes to green jobs. The Environmental Protection Agency (EPA) has its own Office of Water, and several other federal agencies as well as state and municipal departments hire employees specifically to work on water quality. A job in this area could entail developing watersheds, desalinating ocean water, and cleaning and managing wastewater. It also could involve working to preserve and improve the quality of this country's lakes and streams.

The variety of possible careers associated with water is captured admirably by the Work for Water! website (http://workforwater.org/). The site was developed by the American Water Works Association and the Water Environment Federation. If you're interested in a career that focuses on water, you'll find this site invaluable. It contains a list of major jobs in the water field as well as salaries. It also lists programs found at universities and community colleges. There is even a job board to help you find your first job in this field.

The market for hydrologists, including environmental hydrologists and water resource managers, is bright. The U.S. government estimates that these occupations will experience much-faster-than-average growth over the next several years. Keep in mind that this forecast only covers hydrologists and not the entire gamut of water quality occupations.

Whereas research and engineering jobs require university degrees, many jobs in this sector of the economy require only a credential or two-year degree. Table 1.8 lists some typical water quality jobs.

TABLE 1.8: REPRESENTATIVE WATER QUALITY JOB TITLES

Environmental Watershed Planner	Wastewater Plant Operator
Hydrologist	Water Compliance Engineer
Project Manager—Wastewater	Water Conservation Specialist
Soil and Groundwater Technician	Water Reclamation Specialist
Surface Water Hydrologist	Water Resource Engineer
	Water Resources Planner
	Water-Quality Specialist

Green Building and Construction

Although the recent recession put a serious crimp in new home construction, it's only a blip when it comes to the bright prospects for careers in green buildings and green construction. Contractors that specialize in building using green materials and offering homes that place a premium on sustainability point to the fact that the majority of their customers are now much more green-conscious when it comes to planning their homes.

What is a green home? According to the U.S. Green Building Council, green buildings are ones that reduce their negative impact on their occupants and on the environment in five areas: sustainable site planning, safeguarding water and water efficiency, energy efficiency and renewable energy, conservation of materials and resources, and indoor environmental quality.

Painter's Tip: Green building trades also offer retrofitting for existing homes. Retrofitting creates jobs for electricians, insulation workers, roofers, building inspectors, and a wide range of other types of workers.

A wide variety of jobs are associated with green building trades. Architects can become certified and paint themselves green. The same holds true for contractors, designers, engineers, interior designers, property managers, salespeople, and marketing professionals working for green homebuilders. A number of programs are described in Chapter 10 to help prepare you to become part of the green building industry.

Owners of new green homes as well as retrofitted green homes are likely to ask for LEED-certified construction companies. Leadership in Energy and Environmental Design (LEED) refers to an organization that offers guidelines for the construction of green buildings. The U.S. Green Building Council (www.usgbc.org) offers third-party certification that a building meets all requirements to be labeled a LEED building. Therefore, LEED certification is one way for workers with construction experience to paint themselves green.

In addition to LEED certification, a number of universities and community colleges offer degrees and certificates in green construction. One interesting example is an online accelerated 12-week certificate in Green Building offered by Colorado State University. The university states that the program will help participants prepare for the LEED certification exam as well as provide them with the latest information on environmentally sustainable construction. The university also offers certificate programs in Sustainability and the Environment and Construction Management and Green Building.

Certificate programs are perfect for career changers because they are so clearly targeted toward validating a person's specific knowledge in an area in which they do not have work experience. Sonoma State University (California) has a Green Building credential that can be earned after six full days of instruction. At the time we're writing this book, the cost of the credential is around $1,000—just slightly less than the online program at Colorado State University.

While many students taking these classes will be people already in the construction trade, these credential programs are a perfect way for people who have experience in other areas such as sales, training, administration, analysis, and so on to paint themselves green enough to move into the green building industry.

Green Transportation

In the near future, not only will our homes be greener, but so will our entire transportation network. We'll be driving home from our green jobs to our green houses in our new green cars (or at least riding on our green subways).

The Surface Transportation Policy Project (STPP) estimates that for every $1.25 billion invested on safety, traffic, and environment-related transportation projects, 49,800 jobs are created. The Economic Policy Institute has published a report titled "Transportation Investments and the Labor Market," in which it states that each $100 billion invested in transportation infrastructure and in green jobs would expand the economy's annual output by about $160 billion and generate approximately 1.1 million jobs. The vast majority of these jobs would not require college degrees.

We've already talked about two potential sources of green transportation in the near future: biomass in the form of ethanol based on corn and other crops and hydrogen fuel cells. The EPA is also encouraging the development of clean diesel cars, which opens up still another career area.

Painter's Tip: Believe it or not, *bicycle* manufacturers are finding new opportunities as cities embrace this green form of transportation. As the bike industry grows, there will be a need for additional salespeople, assemblers, supervisors, and marketing personnel, as well as financial support people.

The Department of Energy has earmarked funds to encourage cities to transition to clean energy vehicles. That opens up career opportunities in city government for planners, analysts, technical writers, and a variety of other support personnel. The grants fund new jobs to retrofit all kinds of older diesel engines from those powering school buses and trucks to those powering locomotives.

As noted earlier in this chapter, green automobiles will require all kinds of designers, engineers, fleet managers, and so on. It's important to keep in mind, though, that green automobiles are only a *part* of the overall green transportation solution. There will be ample green career opportunities in both the government and corporate worlds to coordinate, plan, and manage public transportation and corporate commuting solutions. Knowledge of green sustainability practices as well as some prior experience doing administrative work could open up a new career in the green transportation industry. Mass-transit systems require administrators, as do corporate commuter programs. New high-speed train systems will require all types of support personnel, including maintenance workers, marketing personnel, and planners.

TransitTalent.com bills itself as "the career hub for public transportation." In fact, it is a wonderful place to explore the types of public transportation jobs that are available as well as the requirements to qualify for them. Table 1.9 provides a sampling of the job titles associated with the mass-transit industry. You can expect increasing funding in the future as this country explores ways to cut back on oil imports. Most of these jobs offer good pay and excellent benefits.

TABLE 1.9: REPRESENTATIVE PUBLIC TRANSPORTATION JOB TITLES

Analyst, Bus Scheduling	Transit Project Manager
Diesel Technician	Transit-Oriented Development Specialist
Light-Rail Power Supervisor	
Rail Transit Systems Engineer	Transportation Planner
Scheduler	Transportation Scheduling Manager
Transit Coordinator	

Ecotourism

The travel industry is about to undergo a profound change. There is a growing trend toward ecotourism. People are becoming more concerned about the environment and want to ensure that their travel reflects these concerns. That means that there will be a need for travel agents who can design trips that have a minimal impact on the environment. It means learning about venues that rely on sustainable energy and preserve natural habitats.

ASTA's (American Society of Travel Agents) Green Program consists of educational and promotional resources that enable travel agents and suppliers to increase their knowledge of travel's impact on the environment and highlight to consumers their commitment to keeping travel an environmentally friendly business. ASTA Green Program members receive a detailed report educating them on how to operate a green travel business and continuous updates throughout the year on the latest environmental knowledge for travel companies. ASTA's research reveals what customers expect when it comes to ecotravel, as seen in the following table.

TABLE 1.10: ASTA'S TOP ELEMENTS THAT MAKE TRAVEL A "GREEN EXPERIENCE" FOR CONSUMERS

Element	% Share of Responses
Ecofriendly hotel (runs on renewable energy sources, recycles, reuses linens instead of washing daily, and so on)	87%
Uses mass transit and/or renewable-energy vehicles	60%
Sources from local businesses	50%
Company donates to green/environmental causes	45%
Carbon-neutral offsets built into pricing	38%
Qualifies for a recognized, third-party green certification	32%
Authentic interaction with locals	31%

A number of community colleges offer certificate programs for people considering becoming an ecofriendly travel agent. A "green" travel agent will have a leg up on competitors. Ecotourism also creates new careers for people interested in working in hotels and environmentally sensitive areas where they can promote concern for the environment while also increasing revenue. Job titles in this emerging career option include sustainable tourism manager, sustainable tour director, ecotourism planner, and ecotour leader.

Green Education and Training

Couple an interest in green issues and a desire to teach and the result is a career educating people about environmental concerns. This career direction can take many turns. Advocacy groups often hire people to give presentations on environmental topics to schools. There also is a need for educators who care about the earth and have a love for nature to share their knowledge with both children and adults. Career options vary widely. You could coordinate living history and interpretive tours, develop environmental education programs, or teach outdoor education and recreation programs. Outdoor educators work at nature centers, parks, and schools. Table 1.11 shows some common job titles in this field.

TABLE 1.11: REPRESENTATIVE GREEN EDUCATION JOB TITLES

Education Director	Outdoor Education Educator
Environmental Educator	Outdoor Education Program Manager
Instructor/Naturalist	Wilderness Therapy Instructor

In addition to teaching positions, people interested in education and the environment can also target careers as environmental trainers. Companies selling green products often need to hire trainers to educate their sales forces. Environmental organizations often hire advocates to make presentations advocating their positions on issues. In many ways these jobs are like teaching jobs, but they don't require filling out report cards.

Painter's Tip: The Environmental Career Opportunities website (www.ecojobs.com) is an excellent place to learn more about the types of jobs available to people who are interested in this career direction. A word of warning, though: This site requires a subscription.

Green Careers Monitoring Environmental Conditions

It's one thing for Congress to pass laws that require environmental regulations; it's quite another thing to make sure these regulations are understood and followed by companies doing business in this country. Environmental regulations will fuel the growth of a significant number of administrative jobs for people to monitor environmental conditions, whether they are within manufacturing plants or within white collar offices.

The many certificate programs listed in Chapter 10 can serve as a gateway to some very interesting careers monitoring environmental conditions. Generally these positions do not require law degrees but do require a college education and some experience performing analysis and planning functions. One very common position is that of sustainability manager, a person responsible for monitoring how successful the company is in meeting its environmental goals. The sustainability manager often serves as a spokesperson for the company on environmental issues. Some of the other growing jobs in this field include compliance lawyers and program managers, emissions certification specialists, and environmental compliance officers.

Green Careers Changing the World

Many people choose a green career because they want to make the world a better place, to keep it clean and safe for future generations. A number of green careers enable you to really feel like you're making a significant difference. Many nonprofit environmental organizations hire advocates. They can have many different titles, including (but not limited to) the following:

- Environmental Advocate
- Environmental Affairs Specialist
- Field Representative
- Grassroots Advocacy Coordinator
- Program Organizer

Following is a typical job description for an environmental advocate showing that they do make a positive difference and have a lot of responsibility:

> The Shareholder Advocate will design and implement strategic campaigns that make the business case for responsible corporate action and have a real impact on the environment. The Shareholder Advocate will also help coordinate XXX's work with that of other responsible investors as well as with the broader community of environmental advocates, researchers, and policy experts.
>
> XXX is seeking a candidate with a demonstrated commitment to the environment, excellent writing skills, exceptional people skills, an appreciation of strategy, a fearless approach to calling members of the media, and a proven ability to juggle multiple projects. The candidate should be able to work effectively in both corporate and nonprofit settings.
>
> Qualifications:
>
> - A demonstrated commitment to environmental issues, and an interest in environmentally responsible businesses and socially responsible investing;
>
> - Strong verbal, writing, interpersonal, strategic, and analytical skills with good attention to detail;
>
> - An ability to work both as part of a team and deliver independent projects;
>
> - Enthusiasm for travel within the U.S.;
>
> - A college degree is required.

As you can see, the educational requirements of the preceding position are such that many career changers would qualify provided they could show sufficient knowledge and interest in the specific environmental issues involved.

Working Close to Nature

When many people think of green careers, they actually imagine themselves out in the woods or on the oceans, protecting the environment on the front lines. Although there are plenty of scientific jobs monitoring and researching environmental conditions that require advanced college degrees, there also are an enormous number of career paths requiring only an undergraduate degree and some green expertise. Careers are available in protecting and managing wildlife habitats and watershed areas, park planning, and environmental restoration. Chapter 10 offers a list of websites that can help you learn more about these various professions.

> **Painter's Tip:** Organic farming is growing in popularity and is one way for enterprising farmers to get even greener. Many consumers are willing to pay a higher price for organic produce, and small and independent farmers are learning how to find that market.

Take the fish industry as an example. Restrictions on deep-sea fishing are likely to increase the need for sustainable aquaculture farm and fish hatchery managers and workers.

Wildlife technicians work in a variety of environments to maintain and preserve wildlife. A recent job posting for a Wildlife Technician described the duties as follows:

> Issue daily and seasonal permits to hunters accessing state-managed lands; take telephone reservations during small-game and archery seasons; respond to public requests for information on hunting and wildlife programs; stock pheasants 1–3 nights and care for birds daily; collect biological data on harvested deer; record and summarize hunter use figures; post boundaries on state-managed lands; repair and maintain pheasant pens and participate in other regional wildlife programs; perform land-management activities including trail maintenance, grassland management, and facility maintenance. The Technician would assist in the regional management of nongame species by erecting bluebird boxes, pre-fencing breeding bird areas, and assisting on tiger salamander surveys.

The educational requirements for such a position are as follows:

> 30 semester credit hours, including 12 semester credit hours in fisheries, marine resources, or wildlife management; mariculture; marine biology; aquaculture; aquatic, marine, or terrestrial ecology; zoology; marine technology; botany; limnology; hydrology; or oceanography.

This type of position represents a "foot in the door" to a new career *outdoors* helping to maintain the balance in nature.

Businesses with a Green Twist

All of the career paths already mentioned are firmly within the new green economy, but there are ways to tap into that market that don't require a specifically green career.

For example, many people dream of starting their own businesses. One way of improving the odds that a new business will be successful is to consider adding a green tint. If you don't have the wherewithal to start your own business, by adding green expertise you could convince a small business owner to give you a chance to appeal to clients who want environmental sustainable solutions. Table 1.12 shows how this is possible.

TABLE 1.12: ADDING A GREEN TINT TO A SMALL BUSINESS

Type of Small Business	Adding a Green Tint
Dry cleaner	Use only environmentally friendly chemicals and processes.
Landscape architect	Specialize in low-water, environmentally friendly designs.
IT specialist	Specialize in data centers that minimize energy usage and virtualized resources.
Accountant	Specialize in environmental accounting.
Farmer	Specialize in organic farming and become part of the buy-it-local movement.
Lawyer	Specialize in environmental law.
Auto mechanic	Specialize in electric cars, fuel cells, and so on.

(continued)

(continued)

Type of Small Business	Adding a Green Tint
Investment advisor	Specialize in investments involving green companies and green technology.
House-cleaning service	Specialize in using only environmentally friendly cleaning supplies.
Printer	Specialize in using recyclable and environmentally friendly materials.

New Green Occupations

Our focus throughout this book is on helping you change careers with minimal disruption in time and income. For that reason, we haven't really discussed a number of careers that require advanced degrees and years of training. Although some readers might be interested in becoming an environmental scientist, a hydrologist, or a geologist, the majority of readers may not be able to pursue the advanced degrees required for these jobs.

When we discuss career tracks later in the book, you'll see that after you have leveraged your educational background and previous job experience, and have credentialed yourself as someone with some green expertise, you can move up the ladder by adding a graduate degree with evening classes while working in your chosen career field. In fact, it's likely your new employer will help pay for that degree.

Regardless of your education or your background, your industry, or your interests, there is a green career out there for you, and one that won't take you long to prepare for.

Following is a list of green occupations compiled by the U.S. government. They are so new that our government has not yet been able to even provide employment projections or wage, education, and training information. Take a look at the list, think about the industries and careers touched on in this chapter, and consider some of the ways you might want to paint your career green. Starting with the very next chapter, we'll show you how to do it.

TABLE 1.13: THE U.S. DEPARTMENT OF LABOR'S LIST OF NEW GREEN OCCUPATIONS

Air-Quality Control Specialists

Automotive Engineering Technicians

Automotive Engineers

Biochemical Engineers

Biofuels Processing Technicians

Biofuels Production Managers

Biomass Plant Engineers

Biomass Plant Technicians

Biomass Production Managers

Brownfield Redevelopment Specialists

Carbon Capture and Sequestration Systems Installers

Carbon Credit Traders

Carbon Trading Analysts

Chief Sustainability Officers

Climate Change Analysts

Compliance Managers

Electrical Engineering Technologists

Electronics Engineering Technologists

Energy Auditors

Energy Brokers

Energy Engineers

Environmental Certification Specialists

Environmental Economists

Environmental Restoration Planners

Financial Quantitative Analysts

Freight Forwarders

Fuel Cell Engineers

Fuel Cell Technicians

Geographic Information Systems Technicians

Geospatial Information Technologists

Geothermal Production Managers

Geothermal Technicians

Green Marketers

Greenhouse Gas Emissions Report Verifiers

Hydroelectric Plant Technicians

Hydroelectric Production Managers

Industrial Ecologists

Industrial Engineering Technologists

Investment Underwriters

Logistics Analysts

Logistics Engineers

Logistics Managers

Manufacturing Engineering Technologists

Manufacturing Engineers

(continued)

(continued)

Manufacturing Production Technicians	Robotics Technicians
Mechanical Engineering Technologists	Securities and Commodities Traders
Mechatronics Engineers	Solar Energy Installation Managers
Methane Capturing System Engineers/Installers/Project Managers	Solar Energy Systems Engineers
Methane/Landfill Gas Generation System Technicians	Solar Photovoltaic Installers
Microsystems Engineers	Solar Power Plant Technicians
Nanosystems Engineers	Solar Sales Representatives
Nanotechnology Engineering Technicians	Solar Thermal Installers and Technicians
Photonics Engineers	Supply Chain Managers
Photonics Technicians	Sustainability Specialists
Precision Agriculture Technicians	Testing, Adjusting, and Balancing (TAB) Technicians
Recycling and Reclamation Workers	Transportation Engineers
Recycling Coordinators	Transportation Planners
Regulatory Affairs Managers	Validation Engineers
Regulatory Affairs Specialists	Water Resource Specialists
Remote Sensing Scientists and Technologists	Water/Wastewater Engineers
Remote Sensing Technicians	Weatherization Installers
Risk-Management Specialists	Wind Energy Engineers
Robotics Engineers	Wind Energy Operations Managers
	Wind Energy Project Managers
	Wind Turbine Service Technicians

Source: CareerOneStop website (www.careeronestop.org/Green Careers) sponsored by the U.S. Department of Labor, Employment and Training Administration.

CHAPTER 2

Careers and Career Changing

Before you decide which is the right new career for you, you should first determine whether you really need to *change* careers or just change the way you think about your current one. To make that decision, you should first consider the significant difference between a job and a career.

Choosing a Path

A job is something you do to earn a living. People often have many jobs in their lives. Sometimes these jobs are in several different career fields. Take Bob, for example. Bob worked as a clerk in a frozen-yogurt store while in high school and worked part-time as a salesman at an electronics store while in college. He majored in political science. In his first job after graduation he worked as a community organizer for an environmental organization. While performing that job, Bob learned some bookkeeping skills and later found a job as an office manager. When he was laid off in his 50s, he found a job as a limousine driver.

Although Bob had many different jobs during his working life, he never really had a coherent set of jobs in a particular field, even though several of his jobs *could* have led to careers. Here are some of the career paths Bob *could* have pursued:

A Sales Career

- Clerk in a frozen-yogurt store
- Part-time sales in an electronics store
- Full-time salesman
- Sales manager
- Regional sales manager
- VP of sales

A Political Activism Career

- Community organizer
- Program director
- Regional director
- National director
- President, nonprofit organization

A Management Career

- Office manager
- District manager
- Regional manager
- Vice president of a company
- President of a company

A Transportation Career

- Limousine driver
- Fleet manager
- Operations manager
- President of the limousine company

Of course, very few of us know from the beginning what career we want to pursue. Even fewer stay in that career path their entire lives. Stan's brother, Paul, knew from the time he was 10 and a paperboy that he wanted to be in the newspaper field. Here's what his career path looked like:

- Paperboy (part-time in elementary school)
- Editor of his high school newspaper
- Obituary writer (part-time) for the city newspaper while in college
- Editor for his college newspaper
- Reporter (full-time) for the city newspaper
- Assistant editor of the city newspaper
- Editor of the city newspaper

Very few of us have that kind of symmetry in our careers. Even if we stay in one career field, that doesn't mean we have to move all the way from entry level to head of the company in order to be happy. Still, a career—by its very nature—means staying focused and using your energy to pursue a related series of jobs within a given field.

Take an elementary school teacher as an example. We'll call her Frieda. Frieda's career *could* have taken this form:

- Kindergarten teacher
- Assistant principal
- Principal
- Assistant superintendent
- Superintendent

Instead, Frieda decided she'd rather work with children than manage adults. She felt dedicated to her profession as a teacher. As a result, her career took the following path:

- Kindergarten teacher
- First-grade teacher
- Third-grade teacher
- Mentor teacher

Frieda grew *within* her given profession by teaching different grades and learning new curricula. Toward the end of her career, her expertise was acknowledged by her selection as a mentor who helped younger teachers learn to be better. Sometimes managing a career means moving up. Other times it means moving over. As long as you are learning and growing as a person and achieving your personal career goals, your career is progressing.

Careers Are More Meaningful Than Jobs

Why bother managing a career? Careers are more meaningful than a series of jobs in different fields for many reasons:

- The more time spent in a given career field, the more knowledgeable an employee is. That makes him or her more valuable and leads to greater income and advancement.

- The more time spent in a given career, the more an employee identifies with that career field. When employees feel that they are part of something much bigger than themselves, there is a feeling of commitment that brings satisfaction.

- Employees in a career field meet likeminded people who often have the same values. These friendships make work more enjoyable and fulfilling. For example, people who decide to become part of a green career field are likely to share key values, such as their desire to preserve the environment.

So as you think about what step to take next, try to think about all of the steps that might come after it.

Think Before You Leap

Often it is not until people are laid off that they realize their jobs were unsatisfying. So if you have been laid off or "downsized," you are now at a crossroads in your life and you have choices. Why not find a job that will complement your interests and aptitude and let you fulfill your passion?

If you are still employed but are unhappy with your current job, you need to do some serious soul searching before deciding to make a career change. Such a change requires a huge expenditure of time and money, so it's important to first examine the reasons you are not happy at work.

Analyzing Your Current Situation

You know yourself better than anybody, so sit down and ask yourself the following questions:

- If you are unhappy because you are bored at work, what makes you bored?

- Is there a way you can work with your boss to restructure your job?

- Would a similar job with a different company bring more satisfaction?

- If you are unhappy at work because of conflicts with fellow employees or your boss, what is the source of these conflicts?

- Is there anything you could do to change the atmosphere and improve your relations with others?

- Is there any reason to believe that the atmosphere would be better at another company if you were performing the same job?

- Are you sure it is the job that is bothering you? Could it be something in your personal life that is carrying over and disrupting your work life?

- Are there other jobs within your given field that you believe you would enjoy and be able to perform effectively?

- Is there another job within your current profession that you could get that would help you eventually gain one of the higher-level jobs that you have identified as a goal?

- Why are you in your current job? What made that job attractive to you originally?

- If you visualize yourself in 10 or 20 years, could you see yourself still working in this same field? If so, what would you be doing?

These questions will get you started thinking about your current situation and where you stand in your career, but they aren't enough to help you plan for the future. For that you must ask yourself some even more fundamental questions, including the following:

- Who am I?

- What can I do?

- Where will I best fit in?

- What do I *need* in a job?

- What do I *want* in a job?

Let's take a look at each of these questions and see how they apply to your choice of career.

Who Am I?

This question prompts you to look at your values and the "big picture" of your life. What are your guiding principles? What is your personal mission statement? What work do you want to accomplish before you die? What do you want to be remembered for? Spend some time answering these questions when you are newly out of work or before you plunge into applying for jobs. Keep in mind, you will find more satisfaction when you fulfill your passion.

What Can I Do?

People enjoy work more if they do something they are good at, if they use their best skills. If you cannot immediately answer what you are good at, you probably need to take an assessment (or test) of your abilities and aptitude. These can usually be given at your local community college, where a counselor can go over the results with you, often at no charge. Just call the campus career center and inquire about such tests. If they aren't available (or there is a fee), there are online aptitude tests you can take. In addition, we have devoted Chapter 3 to helping you assess your strengths and weaknesses in terms of finding the right career.

Where Will I Best Fit In?

What type of company do you want to work for—small, medium, or large? Larger companies often have more upward potential because there are more jobs to move into. But you may be happier in a smaller company where you can make a greater impact. Or you might even want to start your own company. Look at your personality and temperament. Do you need to run the show, or are you happy being a part of the team?

What Do I *Need* in a Job?

Is it a certain amount of money? Flexible hours while you go to school? Do you feel the need to do something challenging and fulfilling? Are you looking for job security? Be honest and address these needs as you pursue your next job.

What Do I *Want* in a Job?

What is it about the job that makes you look forward to going every day? Is it that you enjoy helping people? Do you like to learn new things and solve challenges? Do you like to work outdoors or travel? Think about what your ideal job would look like. How would it be different from jobs you've had in the past?

After you've answered these questions, you'll be better able to steer yourself toward a job that will be satisfying because it will fill your interests *and* meet your needs.

MID-LIFE CAREER CHANGE

No longer do people keep the same job for life. Rather, they change jobs every few years due to economic fluctuations and employment needs. Mid-career and "mature" workers must learn to adjust to shifts in work patterns, flexible schedules, and new responsibilities. They must keep abreast of new technology and methods or risk becoming "dinosaurs" stuck in the same old way of doing things.

The baby boomer generation that has experienced job stability over the past 20 to 30 years is now confronted with early retirement as the digital age comes knocking at their door. A 62-year-old female newspaper national advertising manager that we know with 30 years of successfully selling print advertising was recently let go because it was perceived she didn't know Internet advertising and wouldn't be able to adjust to the change in business strategy. Fifty- and sixty-year-olds (who want and need to work) are being replaced by twenty- and thirty-year-olds who were brought up in the fast-paced, technological world.

But if you are a mid-career changer, don't despair. Just learn to keep up. Take courses in your field to stay current. Attend conferences and workshops. Check with your local library to see whether they offer classes or tutorials on computer programs that you aren't familiar with.

Also keep in mind that some employers welcome mature, seasoned workers who bring excellent work ethics and transferable skills. These experienced workers can be counted on to show up and they know how to treat customers. Your willingness to be a lifelong learner combined with your years of experience can be your greatest asset.

The Right Way to Change Careers

So often the decision to change careers is not an option but a necessity. Either way, it is a decision that deserves your careful attention. You need to explore such considerations as number of years you plan to work, whether your job is still in demand, the amount of money you need to make, potential job satisfaction, and the additional training you might need.

So whether you are looking to shift careers for greater satisfaction, for more money, or to overcome boredom, or if a change of careers is being forced on you, you should know that there is a right and wrong way to change careers. Following are some steps you should take.

Do Your Research

For starters, find companies in industries that you'd like to work for and research them. Study the company's website, read up on it elsewhere on the Internet, and take a look at its last two annual reports. If you know someone working there, ask for an informational interview. Ask them what it's like working there, what type of workers they hire (personality, attitude, aptitude, and so on), what training you'll need to do well in the job, what money you can expect to make, and what a typical day is like on the job.

The more you know about a company, its industry, its competition, and its culture, the better you can position yourself to be what that company wants and needs. We devote a good part of Chapter 6 to providing you with a variety of tools for researching companies, including good questions to ask when interviewing. You can customize your resume and cover letter so that you are exactly what the company is looking for. Then in the interview, you'll need to impress the interviewer with all you know about the company and industry. Most job seekers fail to do this, so you'll have the edge.

Show Your Fit

Learn to describe your previous work experience in ways that are relevant to the kinds of positions you are applying for. Using keywords from the company's job description on your resume and in your cover letter will show that you are a good match. Tell them exactly why your experience (paid and volunteer) equips you to perform the duties of the job. Highlight your accomplishments, awards, and promotions. Employers want capable workers who have been successful in the past to bring those same skills to their company.

Don't Burn Bridges

Finally, whether you are leaving a job on your own or are being asked to leave, be sure to keep the peace. Within an industry, word gets around, and anything negative you said or did as you left your last job could cost you opportunities down the road.

Even if you are changing industries and entering an entirely new career field, you still want to leave your job on good terms. You will probably want a positive recommendation from your supervisor, and your next employers will no doubt ask for references.

Finally, you never know what the future holds. We know of several people who have struck out on a new career path only to return years later to the career they left behind. Keep your options open, even as you follow your dreams.

What Is the Best Career Path for You?

This book is directed at career changers who feel a calling toward a green career, so let's assume that you come to realize that this is the direction you want to go. If so, then you need to consider what a "green" career path for someone with your skills and experience might look like.

Let's examine several different environmental career paths. The point of this exercise is to see how to visualize a career path in a green career field or industry, including the various requirements at each stage necessary for advancement. Where can you find that kind of information?

One excellent place to start is the Bureau of Labor Statistics website (www. bls.gov/green), which contains information on several green careers. There's a brand-new section on careers in wind power, for example. Let's say that you wanted to become a wind turbine service technician. Under "Training and Education," you would find the following information:

The wind energy industry in the United States is relatively young, so there is no one way to be trained as a wind tech. Wind techs need to have mechanical skills and the aptitude to understand how a turbine functions, so some wind techs come from technician jobs in other industries. Experience or training as an electrician also is beneficial.

As formal training programs are developed, employers are placing more emphasis on wind-specific education. Educational institutions—specifically, community colleges and technical schools—are beginning to offer one-year certificate and two-year degree programs in wind turbine maintenance. In certificate programs, students take classes in basic turbine design, diagnostics, control and monitoring systems, and basic turbine repair. For a two-year associate degree, students complete the aforementioned types of classes in addition to general-education courses. Some programs also give students hands-on training and practice on school-owned turbines and machinery.

Although there is no standard certification or course of study, organizations such as AWEA are developing guidelines on the core curriculum and skill sets necessary to work as a wind turbine service technician. AWEA plans to create a list of accredited programs that adhere to a specified curriculum and adhere to certain standards.

In addition to having technical knowledge, wind techs must be physically fit. Climbing up and down the ladders inside turbine towers, even with load-bearing harnesses, can be extremely strenuous. Wind turbine service technicians will often climb several towers during the course of a typical workday, and their bodies, especially their shoulders, must able to withstand this strain.

Source: www.bls.gov/green/wind%5Fenergy/#occusup

So, how does this information help someone plan a career path? It explains that the first step is to find a certificate or two-year degree program at a local community college. In fact, Chapter 10 lists several such programs. Clearly it would be beneficial to find a program that offers hands-on experience operating equipment.

The next step is to consider where a job in this industry might lead you. The American Wind Energy Association (AWEA) is the professional organization for this particular industry. If you search the AWEA's career website (www.careersinwind.com) looking specifically for various wind service turbine technicians, you'll find some that specify that they are *not* entry-level positions. One such job notes that a CCT certification is required. Doing a little research online reveals that CCT stands for a Certified Composites Technician. Clackamas Community College offers such a certificate and notes that "As a CCT, you can use your training to repair wind turbine blades, or move into applications in other industries—automotive, aviation, marine, sports and recreation, research and development, aerospace, and more."

So, someone planning a career path for a wind service technician would list the CCT certificate as a stepping stone to a higher-level position. After several levels of technicians, a final career step could be a *manager* of all those wind service techs. A stepping stone along *that* path probably would include a graduate degree or certificate in management earned part-time after several years as a technician. From there you could keep moving up until you were practically running the place.

In short, the career path for someone interested in wind energy might look like this:

- Entry-level wind service technician
- CCT-certified technician

- Technician manager
- Operations manager

Of course, you should supplement this kind of research with actual interviews with professionals in the field who can provide their own views of what a career path entails. In Chapter 6 we examine how to find key contacts within an industry who can help you learn about that industry.

Painter's Tip: Even though the green industry is relatively new, several professional associations have already been established. These associations are excellent sources of information on the various certificates required as part of a career path.

How Your Career Change Affects Others

Finally, if you are contemplating a career change rather than simply a job shift, you should realize how such a move can affect others, such as your friends and family. For example,

- A career change can be expensive. Even if you continue to work and go to school part-time, there is the cost of tuition, books, and more.

- You will have less time for your family if you have one. Is your spouse willing to accept your being gone evenings and even some weekends? What will the impact be on your children? Have you made some commitments, such as volunteering to coach your daughter's soccer team or work with your son's Boy Scout troop, that you will have to give up?

- Even when you finish your training, your first job might offer less income than your current position. Can your finances handle a cut in salary each month?

Such questions require you to sit down and have a discussion with those who are close to you. Assess the pros and cons of your career change carefully, and be sure you've assessed all the risks before making the move. After all, painting your career green can bring numerous rewards in terms of greater potential income, job security, and increased job satisfaction, but like all investments, it requires time, money and commitment to pay off.

CHAPTER 3

Learning More About Yourself

It has been said, "If you don't know where you are going, any road will get you there." But if you want a more *direct* path to happiness and job fulfillment, you need to know yourself and make a career plan. In fact, self-assessment should be the first step anyone takes before he or she looks for work—whether looking for a first job or making a mid-life career change.

Self-assessment can help you to plan your career path, validate your employment direction, and gauge your potential job satisfaction. In short, you need to match your skills, interests, aptitude, and values with jobs most likely to fit you—jobs that make best use of your talents and passions.

Even as your career direction changes due to job satisfaction (or lack of it), economic trends, or technological advances, there is still a core *you*—a defined, unique individual with motivators and goals steering you through life. You must tap into that defining essence to understand what will make you happy and where you will most naturally fit in. You will be more productive and satisfied when you're challenged with tasks that fit your interests and motivations. This is true of any career you want to pursue, no matter what color it is.

Analyzing Your Accomplishments

Throughout your career you have already accomplished many things that were important to your professional development. Whether your company recognized you or not for a job well done, *you* know when you've done something well. These are your accomplishments, and they provide valuable insight into where your career can go from here.

To a prospective employer, these accomplishments are the best evidence you can give of your demonstrated competencies and strengths. They are the place to look for skills and personal traits that make you valuable and attractive to an employer. Knowing your accomplishments can help you to decide when and where your talents and abilities are best utilized, which, in turn, can help you decide what career move to make.

To get started, try brainstorming a list of your accomplishments. Aim for a dozen. Helpful resources to jog your memory might be previous versions of your resume, written job descriptions, and past performance review evaluations. You can also ask these questions of people who know you personally and professionally:

1. Describe me in one word.

2. What is my greatest strength?

3. What is my biggest weakness?

Being aware of your best skills, personal traits, and the technical knowledge you possess will help you to know what characteristics you value most in yourself, as well as which working environments would be the best fit.

Let's first make some distinctions among skills, personal traits, and technical knowledge:

- **Skills** are learned (through formal education or training) or acquired (through on-the-job experience) and are used to get something done. They can usually be transferred to other types of jobs. Some examples are:

Analyzing	Selling
Calculating	Supervising
Helping	Training
Lifting	Writing

- **Personal traits** are those personal characteristics, either inborn or developed, that tell an employer how you use your skills and how you fit in. Some examples are being

Adaptable	Organized
Calm	Persuasive
Loyal	Resourceful
Motivated	Responsible

- **Technical knowledge** refers to the way each particular company handles information, policies, and procedures. Many times, this information can be picked up very quickly and also can transfer from one job to the next, especially in similar industries. Some examples include

Cost Accounting	Plant Management
Inventory Control	Software Engineering
Market Research	Wage and Salary Administration

To help you in identifying and listing your accomplishments, carefully consider the following questions. Throughout your work experience were there any opportunities when you

- Improved operations by making things more efficient? Saved time? Automated procedures?
- Improved profitability, quality, reliability, or performance?
- Consistently met or exceeded deadlines?
- Reduced downtime or increased productivity?
- Achieved the same or greater results with fewer resources?
- Increased sales/profits or reduced costs?
- Created or developed a new plan, program, procedure, or service?
- Made important contributions to a major group or project?
- Implemented administrative procedures or programs?
- Took initiative in handling a problem with little or no increase in time, money, or staffing?
- Received any awards, commendation letters, merit increases, promotions, bonuses, or other formal recognition?

List as many recent accomplishments as possible. However, any significant achievement, no matter how long ago, is worth including.

Painter's Tip: You may have some accomplishments that you performed *off* the job, through volunteer work or community activities, for example. If so, you could also include these in your list of accomplishments.

Now use the following worksheet to help you analyze your accomplishments. Feel free to use extra paper if you want to analyze more than one.

ACCOMPLISHMENT WORKSHEET

My Accomplishment _____

_____

Problem or situation and why action was required:

_____

_____

_____

Action—Briefly state the key actions you took:

_____

_____

_____

Results—Specify the results achieved. Quantify if possible:

_____

_____

_____

Why is this important to you personally?

_____

_____

_____

List those **skills** used to achieve the results:

_____

_____

_____

_____

(continued)

(continued)

Indicate which of your **personal traits** contributed to this achievement:

_____

_____

_____

_____

What **technical knowledge** or information (policies, procedures, and so on) was applied:

_____

_____

_____

_____

Knowing *how* you achieved your proudest accomplishments will help you as you explore new green career occupations where those same personal assets could be applied.

Knowing What You Have to Offer

Looking back and analyzing your personal accomplishments is just one way to uncover where your career interests and abilities lie. But you have skills and traits that you use every day and values that guide your actions at work. Having a comprehensive understanding of everything you bring to the table will be invaluable as you look to paint your career green.

Following are lists of skills, personal traits, and work values for you to look through. Check those that describe you best. When you have finished, take the time to write down the skills, traits, and values that are most important to you. You will use these later when making a career decision.

SKILLS CHECKLIST

Human Relations Skills

❏ Avoid stereotyping people

❏ Comfortable with different kinds of people

❏ Cooperative team member

❏ Deal effectively with conflict

❏ Establish rapport

❏ Listen intently

❏ Sensitive to others

❏ Tactfulness

❏ Treat people fairly

Helping Skills

❏ Assist people in making decisions

❏ Encourage others to expand and grow

❏ Enhance people's self-esteem

❏ Help people help themselves

❏ Let people know you really care about them

❏ Patient with difficult people

❏ Responsive to people's feelings and needs

Training/Instructing Skills

❏ Create a stimulating learning environment

❏ Create the sense of being part of a caring group

❏ Enable self-discovery, encouraging creativity

❏ Explain difficult ideas and concepts

❏ Perceptively answer questions

❏ Present written or spoken information in a logical, step-by-step fashion

❏ Teach at the student's or group's level

❏ Train people at work

(continued)

(continued)

Leadership Skills

- ❏ A person of vision
- ❏ Accept responsibility for failures
- ❏ Get elected/selected as a group leader
- ❏ Give credit to others
- ❏ Make difficult decisions
- ❏ Motivate/inspire people
- ❏ Open to other people's ideas
- ❏ Perceived as a person with high integrity
- ❏ Reputation for being reliable
- ❏ Settle disagreements

Managing Skills

- ❏ Anticipate problems and prepare alternatives
- ❏ Break through red tape
- ❏ Complete projects on time
- ❏ Establish effective policies/ procedures
- ❏ Find/obtain the resources necessary for a task
- ❏ Gain trust and respect of key people
- ❏ Make effective recommendations
- ❏ Organize projects and programs
- ❏ Set priorities
- ❏ Take the initiative when opportunity appears
- ❏ Work closely and smoothly with others

Supervising Skills

- ❏ Consistently recruit and hire promotable people
- ❏ Create an environment for people to trust and respect each other
- ❏ Delegate work effectively
- ❏ Effectively discipline when necessary
- ❏ Encourage people to want to do their best
- ❏ Know the strengths and weaknesses of others
- ❏ Mediate
- ❏ Reduce turnover
- ❏ Stay in touch/communicate with staff
- ❏ Train and develop staff

Persuading Skills

❒ Close a deal

❒ Effectively sell ideas to top people

❒ Get departments or organizations to take desired action

❒ Get people to change their views on long-held beliefs

❒ Get people/clients/customers to reveal their needs

❒ Help people see the benefits of a course of action

❒ Influence others' ideas and attitudes

❒ Obtain consensus among diverse groups

❒ Sell products, services, or ideas

Financial Skills

❒ Develop a budget

❒ Develop cost-cutting solutions

❒ Gut feeling for financial trends

❒ Manage money/make money grow

❒ Negotiate financial deals

❒ Stay within a budget

❒ Understand economic principles

Mechanical and Tool Skills

❒ Assemble/Build/Install

❒ Do precision work

❒ Drafting/mechanical drawing

❒ Figure out how things work

❒ Invent

❒ Operate machinery

❒ Operate power tools

❒ Troubleshoot/diagnose problems

❒ Understand electricity

❒ Understand manuals/diagrams

❒ Use hand tools

(continued)

(continued)

Idea Skills

- ❏ Able to look beyond the way things have been done in the past
- ❏ Be creative
- ❏ Conceive and generate ideas
- ❏ Find ways to improve things
- ❏ Improvise
- ❏ Recognize new applications for ideas or things
- ❏ See the big picture
- ❏ Synthesize and borrow ideas

Planning Skills

- ❏ Accurately assess available resources
- ❏ Accurately predict results of proposed action
- ❏ Anticipate problems before they develop
- ❏ Determine priorities
- ❏ Develop alternative actions in case the primary plan doesn't work as expected
- ❏ Finish projects on time
- ❏ Plan programs or projects
- ❏ Schedule effectively
- ❏ Set attainable goals

Problem Solving/Troubleshooting Skills

- ❏ Able to come in and take control of a situation
- ❏ Bring order out of a chaotic situation
- ❏ Determine root causes
- ❏ Help a group identify solutions
- ❏ Improvise under stress
- ❏ Not stopping with the first "right" answer that comes to mind
- ❏ Recognize and resolve problems while they're still relatively minor
- ❏ Select the most effective solution
- ❏ Stay calm in emergencies

Researching/Investigating Skills

❏ Able to sift important information from unimportant

❏ Detect cause-and-effect relationships

❏ Develop hypotheses

❏ Develop new testing methods

❏ Follow up on leads

❏ Gather information from people

❏ Know how to find information

❏ Organize large amounts of data and information

❏ Research in a library and online

❏ Weave together threads of evidence

Analyzing Skills

❏ Accurately predict what will occur based on facts, trends, and intuition

❏ Analyze trends

❏ Diagnose needs/problems

❏ Evaluate reports and recommendations

❏ Identify more efficient ways of doing things

❏ Interpret/evaluate data

❏ See both sides of an issue

❏ Simplify complex ideas

❏ Synthesize ideas

❏ Weigh pros and cons of an issue

Organizing Skills

❏ Organize data/information

❏ Organize offices

❏ Organize people to take action

❏ Organize systems

❏ Organize/plan events

(continued)

(continued)

Artistic Skills

- ❏ Calligraphy/lettering
- ❏ Capture a feeling, mood, or idea through drawing
- ❏ Conceive visual representations of ideas and concepts
- ❏ Depth perception
- ❏ Design visual aids
- ❏ Painting
- ❏ Produce high-quality mechanical and line drawings
- ❏ Sense of beauty
- ❏ Sense of color combinations
- ❏ Sense of proportion and space
- ❏ Sense what works and looks right

Observing Skills

- ❏ Eye for fine/small details
- ❏ Hear/see/feel things others are unaware of
- ❏ Highly observant of surroundings
- ❏ Intuitive
- ❏ Perceptive/sensitive/aware
- ❏ Recall names and faces of people

Performing Skills

- ❏ Dance
- ❏ Elicit strong emotions from an audience
- ❏ Make people laugh
- ❏ Model
- ❏ Play musical instruments
- ❏ Poised and confident before groups
- ❏ Read poetry
- ❏ Responsive to audience moods
- ❏ Sing

PERSONAL TRAITS

Look over the following list of personal traits and check the ones that describe you.

❏ Accurate	❏ Efficient	❏ Organized
❏ Adaptable	❏ Empathetic	❏ Patient
❏ Analytical	❏ Energetic	❏ Perceptive
❏ Appreciative	❏ Enthusiastic	❏ Persistent
❏ Articulate	❏ Fair	❏ Persuasive
❏ Artistic	❏ Flexible	❏ Practical
❏ Assertive	❏ Generous	❏ Precise
❏ Calm	❏ Goal-oriented	❏ Productive
❏ Concise	❏ Good listener	❏ Quick learner
❏ Confident	❏ Good memory	❏ Reliable
❏ Conscientious	❏ Hardworking	❏ Resourceful
❏ Considerate	❏ Helpful	❏ Responsible
❏ Consistent	❏ Honest	❏ Responsive
❏ Cooperative	❏ Imaginative	❏ Risk taker
❏ Coordinated	❏ Innovative	❏ Self-confident
❏ Creative	❏ Inquisitive	❏ Sensitive
❏ Decisive	❏ Insightful	❏ Sincere
❏ Dedicated	❏ Instinctive	❏ Tactful
❏ Dependable	❏ Intuitive	❏ Team player
❏ Detail-oriented	❏ Logical	❏ Thorough
❏ Diplomatic	❏ Loyal	❏ Troubleshooter
❏ Discreet	❏ Motivated	❏ Trustworthy
❏ Dynamic	❏ Observant	❏ Versatile
❏ Easygoing	❏ Open-minded	❏ Vibrant

WORK VALUES

Following are common satisfiers that people desire in their work. Rate each of these on a scale from 1 to 4, where 4 is highly important to you and 1 is not important at all.

____ **Aesthetics:** Be involved in studying the beauty of things, ideas.

____ **Affiliation:** Be recognized as a member of an organization.

____ **Artistic/creative:** Engage in creative work in any of several art forms.

____ **Change/variety:** Have responsibilities that frequently change.

____ **Community:** Live in a town where you can get involved in community affairs.

____ **Competition:** Engage in activities where there is a clear win or loss.

____ **Creative (general):** Create new ideas, programs, and so on not previously developed.

____ **Fast paced:** Work where there is high activity and it is fast paced.

____ **Friendship:** Develop close personal relationships at work.

____ **Help others:** Help others in a direct way, individually or in a group.

____ **Help society:** Do something to contribute to the betterment of the world.

____ **Independence:** Working without significant direction from others.

____ **Influence people:** Able to change attitudes or opinions of others.

____ **Intellectual:** Be regarded as an expert in your field.

____ **Knowledge:** Engage in the pursuit of knowledge, truth, and understanding.

____ **Location:** Work close to home in a town that supports your lifestyle.

___ **Make decisions:** Have the power to decide courses of action, policies.

___ **Moral fulfillment:** Feel that work is morally fulfilling.

___ **Power/authority:** You control the work activities/destinies of others.

___ **Precision Work:** Work in situations where there is little tolerance for error.

___ **Profit-gain:** Likely to accumulate much money or material gain.

___ **Public contact:** Have a lot of day-to-day public contact.

___ **Recognition:** Be publicly recognized for good quality of work.

___ **Security:** Be assured of keeping your job and financial status.

___ **Stability:** Have work routine and responsibilities not likely to change.

___ **Supervision:** Be directly responsible for the work done by others.

___ **Time freedom:** Work that can be done on your own schedule.

___ **Work alone:** Do projects alone with little contact from others.

___ **Work under pressure:** Work situations are under time pressure and quality of work is judged critically by others.

___ **Work with others:** Work in a team toward a common goal.

PUT IT ALL TOGETHER

Now look over the previous lists to summarize the skills, personal traits, and work values that you feel are your strongest and want to include as part of your career. List them here:

Skills

_____

_____

(continued)

(continued)

Personal traits

Work values

Congratulations! You've just discovered what motivates you and helps you to achieve success in your work. Finding a position that uses your skills, matches your personality, and supports your work values will give you greater job satisfaction.

Additional Career Assessments

The preceding exercises should have given you enough self-awareness to get started repainting your career. However, some readers may need a little more self-reflection. Most communities have nearby colleges or workforce development centers available to the public. These places usually have or can direct you to a location where you can take assessments and have them interpreted by career professionals. In addition, many of these assessments are available online. Following are just a few of the more common assessments you might consider taking to help you decide on the right career move for you.

MAPP

Assessment.com offers a free but limited online assessment that you can take and get basic results; or you can upgrade and purchase a more complete description for an additional cost. This online test, called MAPP, provides insight in the following areas:

1. **Interest in Job Content** (those tasks that you want to perform): Identifies your motivations and preferences, called "worker traits," in relation to people, creativity, social activities, routine, tools, and equipment.

2. **Temperament for the Job** (how you prefer to perform tasks): Tells you whether you prefer lots of change and variety on the job. Are you persuasive? Do you prefer to work in teams or independently? Are you driven to evaluate and analyze things?

3. **Aptitude for the Job:** Lets the individual see where he or she fits in and would function best with regard to motivation and preference. When a person is highly motivated in an area, he or she is more likely to be trainable and learn the subject content.

4. **People** (how you relate to people): High ratings support "people-intensive" jobs, whereas low ratings support an individual working apart from others or in isolation.

5. **Things:** How you relate to things and manipulate materials, processes, and mechanical objects.

6. **Data:** Identifies preferences, motivations, and priorities for certain mental activities.

7. **Reasoning:** Focuses on where, why, and how thinking will be applied in your prospective career.

8. **Mathematical Capacity:** Looks at how you relate to math. Is it a motivator for you and a vocational interest?

9. **Language Capacity:** Looks at how you relate to the use of language at work.

Myers-Briggs Type Indicator (MBTI)

The Myers-Briggs Type Indicator (MBTI) is a widely used instrument providing four attitudes/psychological functions and a possible 16 personality combinations:

A. Extroverts vs. Introverts

B. Sensors vs. Intuitives

C. Thinkers vs. Feelers

D. Judgers vs. Perceivers

Each of us tends to be more developed in one area of the pair than the other. For example, extroverts are outgoing and gregarious, energized by people, like to speak, and are interested in results. By contrast, introverts are quiet, reflective, and are interested in ideas.

Each of these personality traits and temperaments lead to four personality types—Analyzers, Supporters, Creators, and Directors—that are each best suited for certain careers. Analyzers, for example, would fit well in engineering, mechanical, and technical jobs, whereas supporters would find satisfaction in teaching, social work, nursing, or counseling. Creators make good writers, artists, musicians; while Directors succeed in law enforcement, banking, and outdoor recreation. Knowing your personality preference can be a real asset in choosing a career.

Discover Career Assessment

The Discover Career Assessment examines your interests, abilities, and values based on information you provide about yourself and matches them to specific career areas. It allows you to explore a variety of occupations, majors and schools, salary information, and training requirements. This online assessment requires a user ID, so call your local college and see whether it offers this assessment.

The interest, abilities, and work values inventories can help you learn more about yourself. Results from the abilities inventory will suggest which career areas best fit your abilities. Results from the values inventory will suggest career areas that are more likely to contribute to work satisfaction.

Painter's Tip: After taking whatever assessment you choose, it is a good idea to meet with a career counselor to go over the results and develop realistic career goals. A career counselor can also help you to explore and evaluate what education or training you might need.

Find the Road That Gets You There

In this chapter you have explored your skills, personal traits, temperament, work values, and technical knowledge so that you can make an informed career change. This knowledge, combined with an analysis of your past accomplishments, will help you find a green career that you will be well suited for and satisfied with.

The next chapter will show you how to research the green careers that you are interested in and where to go to find answers to the many questions surrounding your new career choice.

CHAPTER 4

Researching a New Environmental Career

In this chapter, you'll learn how to research a new green career. After all, you can't develop a career-changing plan until you know which career to pursue. To help you, we're going to begin by looking at broad categories of green careers, show you how to narrow these down, and then discuss how to learn more about your chosen career from people already in the field.

In Chapter 1 we pointed out why green jobs are on the rise and discussed several types of green careers in general terms. In this chapter, we take a more detailed look at resources available to help you learn more about these specific career options.

A Checklist for Researching Career Options

Before looking at specific environmental career choices, let's go over some questions to keep in mind.

- **How viable is the career?**

  If you're going to spend money preparing for a career, you need to feel reasonably comfortable that the career you've selected will be viable for several years and will continue to grow at a reasonable rate. Later in this chapter we explain how you can access the U.S. government's forecasts for specific occupations' growth rates.

- **Does the salary range meet your expectations?**

  Career changers generally already have families and responsibilities. Changing a career usually requires some sacrifices by every member of the family. Training costs money and takes you away from the family. So, although a new career likely won't make you rich (at least not at the start), it should provide enough salary that you can live comfortably. If you're leaving a $70,000 job for a new one at $40,000, you have to be sure that everyone in your family can adjust to a new lifestyle and that they've all agreed that the intangible rewards outweigh the loss of some material comforts.

- **Are there geographic limitations?**

  If you're excited about a job in the wind-power industry, do you live in a state where wind power is a viable industry? If not, are you prepared to move to one of the states where there is significant business development in that industry? Is your family willing to pull up roots, find a new church, a new soccer team for your kids, and a new job for your spouse? If so, what are the living costs in the new state and what are the job prospects for your spouse there? These are hard questions, but it's better to ask them now rather than wait until you start to get job offers and realize at that point that you have to move.

Finally, as you move through each green career track, keep in mind all of the work you did in the previous chapters. Ask yourself whether the career you are looking at suits your skills, personal traits, and work values to see whether the kinds of jobs in that industry would be a good "fit" for you.

> **Painter's Tip:** Obviously not all of the careers outlined in this chapter will interest you. If you already know which path your career will take, feel free to jump to that section and start exploring.

Exploring Sustainable-Energy Career Careers

Sustainable energy is hot right now, whether it's solar power, wind power, or biofuel. Let's take them in order and look at ways you can learn more about each career option.

Solar Energy Careers

The Solar Energy Industries Association's (SEIA) website (www.seia.org) is an excellent starting point for researching careers in that field. It has a section entitled "Solar Jobs Spotlight" that includes profiles of dozens of people with different job titles working in the solar industry, including the name of the company where the person works—making this one potential source for informational interviews. The website also has a jobs board with more than 1,000 solar-specific job openings. It's helpful, as an example, to learn what a marketing manager does for a solar company, or what the specific duties are for a solar program director.

JobMonkey.com is another site that has valuable information on different solar power career options (www.jobmonkey.com/greenjobs/solar-energy.html). You can find more solar jobs to examine at the Jobs in Solar Power website: http://jobsinsolarpower.jobamatic.com/a/jobs/find-jobs.

The California Employment Development Department's website is adding green occupational guides that might be of interest. Its first occupational guide is for Solar Thermal Installers and Technicians. Although the opportunities discussed are specific to California, the guide contains excellent information on the tasks to be performed, the likely salary, training required, and so on. Read this guide at www.calmis.ca.gov/file/occguide/solar-thermal-installers-green.pdf.

Another good way to learn about a career—and make contacts with people in the know—is to attend conferences. The American Solar Energy Society holds an annual conference. At the Solar 2010 conference in Phoenix, Arizona, there were plenty of exhibits as well as a career center specifically for people interested in solar careers. You can learn more about the next one at www.nationalsolarconference.org.

Finally, the Green Careers Guide website has a section on solar power. Included is an article on ten rising solar careers (www.greencareersguide.com/10-Rising-Solar-Careers.html). It's an excellent description of positions that vary widely in terms of educational requirements—from solar operations engineers, to solar panel installers, to solar sales representatives. The site has links for each career with information on the educational requirements, career outlook, salary, and a description of "What kind of person is good at this position?"—ideal for matching careers to your own skills and abilities.

Wind Power Careers

The American Wind Energy Association has created a centralized website just for industry career information: www.careersinwind.com. It promises in the near future to add content on how to apply transferrable skills to changing careers and move into a wind energy position. The site already contains a job board that can be very helpful because of the descriptions of wind energy jobs.

One of the most complete job boards for wind energy is the Simply Hired website, which trolls through the Internet gathering wind power jobs wherever it finds them. When we examined this website, it listed more 4,000 jobs in the wind industry: www.simplyhired.com/a/jobs/list/q-wind+energy.

Yet another wind employment site with a large job board is WindJobs.org (www.windjobs.org). What makes this site valuable is that it allows for searching in a variety of ways, including searches by salary, state, and country.

For an excellent description of the wind industry and a lengthy listing of wind energy jobs as well as links to educational programs, see the Department of Energy's brochure: www1.eere.energy.gov/library/pdfs/wind_green_jobs_fs.pdf. Finally, one of the very best places to learn about actual wind-power careers is a 2009 article in Renewable Energy World entitled "Eight Careers in Wind Farm Development." The article provides good information as well as quotes from people already doing this work. Read the article at www.renewableenergyworld.com/rea/news/article/2009/09/seven-careers-in-wind-farm-development.

Biofuel Energy Careers

If you are interested in researching careers in biofuel, you might start with the 25-page report on the biofuels job market available at http://jobsinbiofuels.com/biofuels-job-market-report.pdf. The report even has links to the sites of major companies in the biofuels industry that might be hiring.

Afterward you can visit Biofuels Digest (www.biofuelsdigest.com). The site has an excellent job board with very detailed job descriptions, including the education and work experience required. It is possible to filter your searches to look for only engineering positions, analysts, financial, and various other combinations. The vast majority of positions require a bachelor's degree, although some jobs require only an associate degree. You'll see that chemical engineers are in demand, but keep in mind that biofuel companies require project managers, planners, sales managers and representatives, and financial and marketing personnel.

It is in these latter types of positions that we see where transferrable skills from other careers pay immediate dividends. Often it only takes a desire to learn more about the industry for an accountant, manager, marketer, or computer specialist to break into a green career.

The federal government is an excellent source of green careers. The Department of Agriculture, for example, has a sustainable biofuels research unit. It hires support personnel in a number of areas, including finance and administration. However, the bulk of its employees have scientific titles, including the following:

- Agricultural Engineer
- Biological Science Lab Technician
- Biologist
- Chemical Engineer
- Chemical Engineer Technician
- Chemist
- Cost Engineer

- Industrial Equipment Mechanic
- Lab Technician
- Mechanical Engineer
- Outdoor Environmental Careers
- Physical Science
- Plant Physiologist
- Research Chemist
- Research Food Technologist

Finally, JobMonkey.com has a web page on biofuel (www.jobmonkey.com/greenjobs/biofuel.html) that includes information on job growth in this industry (25 to 50 percent over the next decade) as well as educational resources and lists of leading companies.

Exploring Outdoor Environmental Careers

If you'd rather be out *in* Mother nature rather than analyzing her in a lab or converting her into energy in a plant, you should check out the University of Manitoba's Career Centre's website (www.umanitoba.ca/student/counselling/spotlights/environ.html). It includes links to detailed information on the following careers:

- Conservation Officer
- Environmental Engineer
- Geologist

- Hydrologist
- Meteorologist
- Soil Scientist

In addition, the website includes links to virtually every major North American environmental career website.

If you are particularly woodsy, the Global Association of Online Foresters has an excellent website to help career seekers determine whether forestry is the right choice for them (www.foresters.org/careers/index.htm).

Environmental Career Opportunities (ECO) has a subscription website that includes a Natural Resource and Conservation Jobs section as well as an Outdoor and Environmental Jobs section. Typical jobs listed in these sections range from park ecologist to environmental restoration team member to conservation educator.

Finally, the Cyber-Sierra Center for Natural Resources, Forestry, and Conservation website (www.cyber-sierra.com) contains a wealth of information for job seekers interested in working outdoors.

Exploring Government Career Options

As we mentioned before, the federal government is one of the biggest employers of "green" workers. The University of Wisconsin's Department of Environmental Studies has an excellent website (www.uwosh.edu/es/jobs/environmental-jobs-in-the-federal-government) that provides information on environmental jobs with the federal government. It spells out the different levels of service, discusses the ways you can search the U.S. government website for jobs based on different criteria, and even explains the federal internship program, something that might prove very helpful for career changers with valuable work experience and transferrable skills.

Painter's Tip: The federal government has a complex array of qualifications for different levels. The specific qualifications for each level differ depending on the job. Entry-level jobs for people without graduate schoolwork or specialized experience are usually GS-4 (which expects at least two years of college education) and GS-5 (which expects a bachelor's degree).

Table 4.1 shows the number of environmental sciences federal government positions by field in 2010. Table 4.2 reveals the total number of federal government workers in environmental positions by federal agency.

TABLE 4.1: ENVIRONMENTAL SCIENCES FEDERAL POSITIONS BY FIELD

Field	Full-Time Permanent Employees
Forestry Technician	10,453
Environmental Protection Specialist	5,936
Park Ranger	5,322
Soil Conservation	4,145
Fish Biology	2,482
Wildlife Biology	2,463

TABLE 4.2: ENVIRONMENT SCIENCES FULL-TIME POSITIONS BY U.S. FEDERAL AGENCY

Agency	Full-Time Positions
Department of Agriculture	3,479
Department of the Interior	12,583
Department of Defense	6,217
Environmental Protection Agency	5,475
Department of Commerce	2,447
Department of Health & Human Services	1,771
Department of Transportation	1,753
Department of Energy	830
Department of Homeland Security	150

Source: Fedscope, March 2010

This shows both the sheer number and scope of positions within the U.S. government and why it is an option worth researching as you look toward a green career.

Exploring Grassroots Community Career Options

One green career area that allows career changers to feel they really are making a difference is that of environmental advocate. Although some policy advocates work in Washington, D.C., the majority of environmental activists work at the grassroots level. The career ladder generally starts at the local level, moves to the regional level, and peaks at the national level. Many career changers move into this career by beginning with volunteer work to build experience.

One way to discover the best match for you when it comes to volunteering for an environmental organization is to look at the EnviroLink website (www.envirolink.org). The categories it lists range from environmental education to habitat conservation, from waste management to water quality. Whatever your interest, there is an organization out there that needs your help.

Volunteering while pursuing additional training could be a key part of your overall plan for making a career change. The kinds of experience that can help launch you in your career as an environmental activist would include project management, fundraising, organizing/managing volunteers, and meeting with local legislators and other city and state officials.

If you look at the following job description for a Community Organizer, you can see how volunteer work can help prepare you for such a career:

Clean Water Action and Clean Water Fund are looking for an experienced organizer with a track record of success working on community and/or environmental campaigns.

Qualifications:

- Paid or volunteer experience in issue organizing or community/neighborhood-based campaigns. Must have experience in community outreach and campaign strategy and development. Over one year's paid experience preferred.
- Strong oral and written communication skills.
- Experience with canvas programs and/or environmental issues desirable.

Looking at the job description, it's clear that a year or two of volunteer work would give you the experience you need to embark on a career in environmental activism.

Exploring Green Transportation Options

There are a number of excellent sources when it comes to exploring green transportation career options. In Chapter 1 we referred to TransitTalent. com (www.transittalent.com), which bills itself as "the career hub for public transportation." In fact, it is a wonderful place to go to explore the types of public-transportation jobs that are available, as well as the requirements to qualify for them.

A report prepared for the Natural Resources Defense Council (NRDC), United Auto Workers (UAW), and the Center for American Progress in 2010 entitled "Driving Growth: How Clean Cars and Climate Policy Can Create Jobs" (www.americanprogress.org/issues/2010/03/pdf/driving_growth.pdf) describes how new jobs can be created as Americans decrease their dependence on foreign oil. The report forecasts job growth in several different clean vehicle technologies. For example, nearly 20,000 new jobs could be created by 2014 that are specific to full hybrid technology. This number jumps to nearly 43,000 by 2020. As of 2008, there were only 3,014 jobs related to this technology.

Another category that is expected to see big increases is clean diesel. This sector already has a jump on the full hybrid sector with more than 12,000 jobs in 2008. This number is expected to jump to 33,000 by 2014 and more than 42,000 by 2020.

Painter's Tip: For career changers anxious to catch the green transportation wave, it is important to investigate careers in automobile engineering technology. Such a career path generally requires a two-year community college credential, though it might require less time if you already have college credits that can be transferred.

Geography is a key consideration for those breaking into the transportation industry. The report estimates that many of the jobs, especially those in diesels and transmissions, could be concentrated in the Michigan, Indiana, and Ohio regions.

There should be ample career opportunities for career changers who become knowledgeable in electric car and truck fleet management and maintenance as well. There are signs that Fortune 500 companies are beginning to convert their fleets to electric technology. One example is the Frito-Lay division of Pepsi. It recently announced its intention to build the largest fleet of commercial all-electric trucks in North America. Using a grant from the New York State Energy Research and Development Authority, Frito-Lay will deploy 176 electric trucks—and in the process, eliminate the need for 500,000 gallons of fuel annually.

Another place to learn more about the exciting career possibilities of electric car technology is the Electric Drive Transportation Association (www. electricdrive.org). This website includes information on hybrids, hybrid plug-ins, fuel cells, and extended-range electric vehicles. Also take a look at the Rocky Mountain Institute (www.rmi.org), a think tank that focuses on trying to solve the problem of our dependence on oil. The Library section of its website offers a number of fascinating documents that show just how broad the green transportation market is likely to become. It includes reports on green airplanes, greener trucks, and even hydrogen cars.

The key to preparing for a green transportation career, of course, is to find programs that offer forward-looking academic programs. One example is Cerritos College in greater Los Angeles and its automotive training technology program. Cerritos offers certificates, degrees, and special programs in the disciplines of automotive repair, advanced transportation technology, auto collision repair, intelligent transportation systems, and alternative fuel and hybrids, making it one of the most comprehensive programs in the U.S.

Exploring Green Business

If you're considering creating or working for a green business, you can start by becoming part of an online community of green business entrepreneurs. The Green Business website (www.greenbusiness.net) costs $12 per month for a subscription, but it offers the opportunity to communicate directly with people who are creating green businesses. There is a free trial option, so you can see whether it provides the kind of practical advice you need.

Another website of value for green marketers and businesspeople is GreenBiz.com (www.greenbiz.com). This free site offers blogs, news, information on professional organizations, newsletters, and a job board, with focuses on energy and climate, design and packaging, small businesses, business operations, resource efficiency, and marketing and communications.

Green business and nonprofit organizations always have a number of entry-level jobs in which transferrable skills developed in other careers can be leveraged to grab that first rung in the new career ladder. Many nonprofit organizations advertise entry-level positions that require communications, organizational, and analytical skills that can be developed outside of a green field.

A GREEN JOB FOR EVERYONE

When people think of "green jobs" or "green careers" they normally think of scientists and researchers, chemical engineers or plant managers. They don't think about the millions of other workers required to keep the "green economy" running: the accountants and auditors, the sales managers and representatives, the website developers and public relations specialists. But green jobs are everywhere, and odds are good that whatever jobs you've had in the past have a "green" equivalent, or at least something close. You just have to find it.

To get an idea of how easy it is to leverage your transferrable skills to slide into a new green career, let's look at an Energy Analyst opening, a mid-level green corporate job from the Green Dream Jobs website (www.sustainablebusiness. com). The job requires two years' of "related professional experience" and an undergraduate college degree. Required work tasks include:

- Conduct statistical analysis including the ability to calculate means and standard errors and to run multivariate regressions.
- Analysis of data to address research questions outlined in project plans.
- Manage multiple tasks and projects.
- Assist with data management and analysis.
- Document procedures and results. This involves recording the steps taken to arrive at an end result so that results can be recreated.
- Technical writing skills. Summarize results in writing.
- Communicate progress and results to other project team members.
- Assist with literature reviews.
- Help in putting together data collection instruments, such as drafting telephone surveys.
- Present data and conclusions of research to project stake holders.

The interesting thing to note is that none of these requirements are specifically green. A person who has held any job with analytical or statistical job duties probably would qualify, particularly if that person had an appropriate green credential.

Researching Green Jobs In-Depth

When researching green careers, it's helpful to use the various career development websites we've mentioned to help you collect a list of job titles that sound intriguing. But they often don't have *all* the facts. You need to do a little more research in order to make the most informed decision possible.

O*NET: Answers to Most of Your Questions

Let's say that you've determined that you want to do something in the sustainable energy field, and you have a list of possible occupations to pursue. Of course you still have lots of questions that need answering if you're to narrow down this list, including

- What are the minimal educational requirements for a position?
- What specific tasks would you be doing on a day-to-day basis?
- What tools and technology would you be required to use on the job?
- What specific job-related knowledge would you be expected to have?
- What kind of mental and physical abilities are required?
- What would the work environment be like?
- What work styles are most important for this occupation?
- What work values are important in this occupation?
- What are the average wages, the number of people currently employed in this occupation, and the projected growth rate?

For a great number of green careers, the best single source of such information is the O*NET Online database (online.onetcenter.org). O*NET is a creation of the U.S. Department of Labor Employment and Training Administration. Under the "Browse Careers" tab is a Green Economy Sector option providing information on more than 200 green careers in 12 different sectors:

- **Agriculture and Forestry:** Includes careers related to using natural pesticides, efficient land management or farming, and aquaculture.

- **Energy and Carbon Capture and Storage:** Includes careers related to capturing and storing energy and/or carbon emissions, as well as technologies related to power plants using the integrated gasification combined cycle (IGCC) technique.

- **Energy Efficiency:** Includes careers related to increasing energy efficiency (broadly defined), making energy demand response more effective, constructing "smart grids," and so on.

- **Energy Trading:** Includes careers related to buying and selling energy as an economic commodity, as well as carbon trading projects.

- **Environment Protection:** Includes careers related to environmental remediating, climate change adaptation, and ensuring or enhancing air quality.

- **Government and Regulatory Administration:** Includes careers related to solid waste and wastewater management, treatment, and reduction, as well as processing recyclable materials.

- **Green Construction:** Includes careers related to constructing new green buildings, retrofitting residential and commercial buildings, and installing other green construction technology.

- **Manufacturing:** Includes careers related to industrial manufacturing of green technology as well as energy efficient manufacturing processes.

- **Recycling and Waste Reduction:** Includes careers related to solid waste and wastewater management, treatment, and reduction, as well as processing recyclable materials.

- **Renewable Energy Generation:** Includes careers related to developing and using energy sources such as solar, wind, geothermal, and biomass. This section also includes traditional, non-renewable sources of energy undergoing significant green technological changes (for example, oil, coal, gas, and nuclear).

- **Research, Design, and Consulting Services:** This sector encompasses "indirect jobs" to the green economy that includes activities such as energy consulting or research and other related business services.

- **Transportation:** Includes careers related to increasing efficiency and/or reducing environmental impact of various modes of transportation including trucking, mass transit, freight rail, and so on.

Now let's assume that you've read about energy auditors, and given your previous work experience and transferrable skills, this occupation sounds interesting. When you select "Energy Auditor," O*NET provides you with a report. First of all, you'll learn that there are a number of job titles corresponding to Energy Auditor including Energy Rater, Energy Consultant, Home Performance Consultant, Building Performance Consultant, and Home Energy Rater. These alternative occupation titles are important because you might see credential programs or jobs on job boards under these terms rather than the Energy Auditor description.

The O*NET online website provides 2009 median wages for an Energy Auditor ($60,610) as well as a projected growth rate (2008–2018) of 7%–18%, definitely faster than the average occupation. The report reveals that although roughly half (49%) of energy auditors indicated they had a bachelor's degree or higher. A third (33%) only reported having had some college classes—good news for career changers who don't want to go back to school for a whole new degree.

Of course, we're only using energy auditor as an example of what the O*NET can do for you. In addition to salary projections, you'll learn what specific tasks are associated with an occupation, what aspects of the work jobholders enjoy, and what aspects of an occupation are most challenging.

The O*NET does not cover every occupation, particularly because many green occupations are just now being created. Still, it is remarkably complete. Let's say that you're intrigued with the concept of biomass and biofuel. When you search the O*NET online, you'll discover the following related job titles:

- Biofuels Production Manager
- Biofuels/Biodiesel Technology and Product Development Managers
- Biofuels Processing Technicians
- Biomass Plant Technicians

In the case of a Biofuels Production Manager, the O*NET uses its orange coding to indicate that this occupation has a bright outlook, meaning it has faster-than-average job growth or at least will result in a significant number of new jobs (100,000 or more).

You'll find that most of the green careers described in the O*NET database are coded orange, which means that your future in just about any green career would have a bright outlook.

Using CareerOneStop

The United States Department of Labor (DOL) has created a website that consolidates several valuable sources of career information. Known as CareerOneStop, it is where the DOL has assembled occupational, demographic, and labor market information at the local, state, and national levels, and thus is a must-use resource as you explore your green career options. What is particularly valuable is that the information on specific occupations can be examined for a particular state. In other words, you can learn what the prospects are for a particular type of work in Texas as well as what specific training programs are available there.

Painter's Tip: It is impossible to keep up with the proliferation of new green careers. In fact, the CareerOneStop website identifies more than a 100 of their green careers as "new." From Brownfield Redevelopment Specialists to Precision Agriculture Technicians, it seems every month brings an occupation that never existed before.

Using this website to explore green careers (www.careeronestop.org/ GreenCareers/ExploreGreenCareers.aspx), you will find lists of occupations within the O*NET's 12 sectors, with an indication of the educational and work experience required for each. Clicking on a sector and then on an occupation of interest brings you to a list of states. Selecting a state provides a career profile for that occupation including an in-depth job description, an informational video (in some cases), and both state and national wages and employment trends. In addition, each description provides links to other sources of information and a list of related occupations. In short, the description and data provide nearly everything you need to decide whether this is a viable career option for you.

The website also enables you to select training programs. You can select from college programs or short-term programs (one to two years). Using the "Education and Training" finder you can specify how long you want the program to be and what state you want to study in. You will then be directed to college programs that meet your needs.

GETTING CERTIFIED FOR A GREEN CAREER

One of the main premises of this book is that many green occupations do not require years of graduate training. In fact, many lucrative and interesting green jobs only require specific credentials that can be earned in relatively short periods of time. The lists of occupations offered through the CareerOneStop website indicate which jobs require such credentials. Clicking on the certification check mark beside one of these jobs leads to a list of certificates, the name of the certifying organization, and links to the organization's website. This is an easy way to not only find jobs that you can qualify for quickly, but the programs that can help you do so.

A Valuable Canadian Resource

The employment section of Eco Canada's environmental careers website (www.eco.ca/default.aspx) requires registration, but it is great for learning which environmental careers match most closely to your background and skills. You can explore careers from 60 occupational profiles using the "Find your ideal career" tool. The tool allows you to search for careers by work preference, education area, or interest.

For example, the "work preference" option displays a list of around 15 attributes. After selecting your own preferences, the site provides a list of matching occupations. Clicking on the occupation itself leads to a menu offering a wide range of information, including a snapshot overview, job duties, career path, essential skills and environmental competencies required, a personal profile, and related profiles.

The "personal profile" option is especially valuable as it provides a report of someone working in that occupation, including the person's career path, a description of a typical day at work, and advice on how to succeed in that career. This type of detail makes a possible new career seem much more tangible and helps career changers narrow down their options.

Visiting the Environmental Career Center

The Environmental Career Guide (www.khake.com/page46.html), sponsored by the Vocational Information Center, is crammed with valuable information on environmental careers. It describes itself as "an education directory that provides links to online resources for career exploration, technical education, workforce development, technical schools and related vocational learning resources."

The links range from professional associations offering career tips to state vocational workforce development sites offering occupational information. The link for geoscientist, for example, takes you the American Geological Institute's excellent website for students and others interested in geological careers. If you don't know where to start researching the green jobs that interest you, the Environmental Career Guide is worth a visit.

Regardless of what field you want to get into, there are dozens, if not hundreds of resources at your fingertips to help you. Just visiting websites is not enough, though. If you really want to discover what it's like to work in a green job, you need to ask someone who is doing it.

USING PROFESSIONAL ASSOCIATIONS AS A RESOURCE

Professional associations are excellent places to learn about environmental careers. Following are just a few that might interest you:

- **The American Academy of Environmental Engineers (www.aaee.net):** Includes a career center link where you can read a description of the environmental engineering occupation including compensation information. There is also a job board where positions are described in detail.

- **The University of Michigan's Multicultural Environmental Leadership Development Initiative (meldi.snre.umich.edu/resources/resource/ Other+Environmental+Professional+Associations):** Includes a lengthy list of links to environmental associations.

- **The Centers for Ocean Sciences Education Excellence (www. oceancareers.com/2.0/index.php):** Offers information on more than 50 ocean-related occupations. You can browse occupations based on the kinds of things you like to do, such as work on ships or work with animals.

- **The Soil Science Society of America (www.soils.org/careers):** The Career Placement link provides profiles of people already in the field, career brochures, and information on compensation.

- **Work For Water (www.workforwater.org):** For people interested in water environmental careers. Offers valuable career information for high school and vocational tech and college graduates, people with advanced degrees in science, as well as military second-career candidates. Included are salary information, specific job tips, and information about scholarships and internships.

The Value of Informational Interviews

As you search through the occupational reference materials described in this chapter, you're bound to have questions. Changing careers is a huge decision, and you want to make sure you have all the facts. That's why it's best to talk to someone in the know.

An informational interview is an interview you have with someone already working in the field you're considering. It's a chance to learn information that you can only get from someone "on the inside." Someone already working in the green field you're considering can help you by answering a number of questions. Here are some examples:

- How do you best prepare for this type of job?

- What is a typical career path? How rapid is promotion?

- What kinds of skills are required to be successful?

- If this person was starting this career over again, is there anything he or she would do differently?

- What does the person like best about the job? What is the least pleasant part of the job?

Identifying People for Informational Interviews

Earlier in this chapter, we pointed out several websites that profiled people already performing various green jobs. These profiles also include the names of the companies where these people worked. That's a good starting point to identify people to talk with. You can also use job openings to identify major companies in specific green fields. Checking the press releases from such companies (found on their websites) will provide a list of public relations (PR) contacts. The PR contact can then help set up an interview with someone in the company.

If you attend a conference or trade show, you'll probably receive a directory of companies attending along with contacts for each company—you might even meet someone who you'd like to interview with. Another excellent source of contacts is the local branch of national industry associations. If you contact an officer in the local chapter of a solar or wind professional association, for example, that person generally will be more than happy to set up an interview for you with someone in that industry.

79

Preparing for an Informational Interview

The best way to prepare is to do your homework. Look over the career information and websites we've listed earlier in this chapter and familiarize yourself with the terminology and trends associated with the career. Look at the website of the company where your interviewee works and read several of the press releases to see what the company considers to be major news.

> **Painter's Tip:** If there appears to be some consolidation taking place in the industry, with bigger companies snapping up smaller ones, be sure to ask about this. It could have an impact on your future prospects and long-term job stability.

The Informational Interview Process

A good informational interview is one in which you and your interviewee both have plenty of opportunity to talk. If the interviewee winds up giving you a lecture on career opportunities, you will walk away frustrated. Similarly, if you dominate the interview and talk too much about your background, then you won't learn much about the career.

Be sure to explain your goal clearly at the beginning of the interview. Make it clear that this is not a veiled attempt to get a job. You are just starting your research and you need help understanding this new career from an insider's perspective. (That doesn't mean you can't return to this person when you finally are in the job-hunting mode, of course.)

Before the interview, spend some time thinking through your answers to some basic questions the interviewee is bound to ask *you*. Some of the more obvious questions include the following:

- Why are you thinking about changing careers?
- What makes this new career appealing to you?
- What have you learned so far about this new career?
- What sorts of things do you enjoy doing at work?
- What, if anything, do you know about this company?

Painter's Tip: Plan on dressing as you would for a job interview. You want to put your best foot forward and leave a favorable impression.

Finally, it may seem old-fashioned to sit down and write a real ink-and-paper thank-you note after the interview, but it's the right thing to do. Remember, you might very well want to talk with this person later when you're closer to looking for your first job in this new career field, so you want your interviewee to think well of you.

As you can see, there are a variety of ways to learn more about specific green jobs. You can use the Internet to do your research, you can volunteer and gain hands-on experience, and you can conduct informational interviews with people who already are employed in green careers. Although all these approaches work well individually, they are even more powerful in combination.

A painter doesn't just choose any color and slap it on the walls, and neither should you. It's critical that you spend some time researching the various green occupations you're considering. In the next chapter we'll help you turn the fruits of that research into a plan that will guide you into your new career.

CHAPTER 5

Developing a Plan

In previous chapters you have explored the many options for painting your career green. Hopefully you have some idea of the kind of work you would like to do. Now comes the hard work of making that career change—and for that you'll need a plan.

You Need Goals, Not Wishes

It is one thing to wish things were different and quite another to set about changing your life and your career direction. To make an effective career transition, you need to turn those wishes into clear, attainable goals.

Do you know the difference between a "wish" and a "goal"? A wish is something desired. By contrast, a goal is something you move toward steadily, facing a series of obstacles and working to overcome them. For example, you might *wish* you were an engineer designing electric cars, but that won't make it so. There are steps involved, including getting the required education and training, researching the companies that invest in that kind of technology, and building up your network and resume so that you can land that job and meet that goal. Reaching a goal requires careful planning: As the saying goes, "If you fail to plan, you plan to fail."

> **Painter's Tip:** Tell everyone you know what your goal is. That way, your friends, relatives, and workmates will encourage and motivate you to achieve it.

All too often, people are forced into a career change and go into their job search without any sense of direction. You would be surprised how many people come into the career center and sit at the computer all day long looking up and applying to jobs on the Internet. That is the extent of their job search and they are surprised when months fly by with still no job offers. Instead, you should tailor your job search to your specific needs and work your network of friends and associates who can help refer you to openings. In short, you need a systematic approach to meeting your career objective. The person who usually gets the job is the one who "works the plan," not necessarily the smartest or the most qualified.

Take Charge of Marketing Yourself

The secret is to take control of your life and your career and to make something concrete happen rather than drift along and let fate determine your path. As we've shown in previous chapters, there are plenty of opportunities out there for people looking to paint themselves green, but they probably aren't going to fall into your lap. You need a plan, and to succeed at that plan, you need to review what you do best, research what education or training is needed to make your previous skills compatible with green market demands, and learn how to market those skills to an employer.

Making Your Skills Work for You

In Chapter 3 you took the time to assess your skills, attributes, preferences, and values. Now it's time to use that knowledge to set career goals.

From an employer's perspective, your skills are the ticket to a job. Matching your specific skill set to what employers are looking for isn't always easy, however. In fact, surveys of employers have verified that only a small percentage of people interviewed have a clear understanding of their specific skills. Even if they do have some idea as to what their strengths are, employers tell us that most job seekers don't present those skills effectively.

To make an effective transition, you need to know how the skills you've acquired in past jobs translate to the green career you want to start. In order to do that, it can be useful to divide those skills into three basic types: transferable skills, adaptive skills, and job-related skills.

Transferable Skills

Transferable skills are general skills that can be useful in a variety of jobs and can be easily transferred from one job or career to another. For example, the ability to write well or to organize and prioritize tasks would be desirable in most jobs. Transferable skills "are skills you have acquired during any activity in your life—jobs, classes, projects, parenting, hobbies, sports—virtually anything that are transferable and applicable to what you want to do in your next job," explains Katherine Hansen, Ph.D., in her article, "Strategic Portrayal of Transferable Job Skills is a Vital Job Search Technique."

In many ways, these skills are your key to a successful career transition because they enable you to move from one *type* of job to another. This is critical when you're thinking about a new "green" career. For example, your leadership and management skills successfully applied in your last company will also serve you well in your upcoming green job.

As we've seen when we've looked at green job descriptions, the difference between a regular job and its "green" equivalent is often just an eagerness to learn about new technology and work towards environmentally beneficial goals. In other words, many times your transferable skills can help you land your new job. After you're there you can learn the more specific skills that make the job "green."

Adaptive Skills

Adaptive skills are the skills you use every day to help you adjust to a variety of situations. They could be considered a part of your personality. Examples of adaptive skills valued by employers include punctuality, honesty, enthusiasm, and interacting well with others. Employers look for these skills in candidates as evidence of how they will fit into the organization.

Although some of these skills are required by *all* employers (like showing up to work on time every day) other adaptive skills hold more value from industry to industry. Sometimes a particular kind of work has its own culture regardless of what company is involved.

For example, one of us (Stan) spent time working closely with software engineers. Interpersonal skills were not particularly prized or apparent in this crowd. Most people talked infrequently as they focused on their programming. Somebody who is considered very social, for example, and who finds great delight in setting up company picnics, planning the company holiday party, or organizing buddy programs for new employees would find working with software engineers very challenging. So consider your adaptive skills carefully when you try to decide whether or not you're a good fit for a particular green company's "culture."

Job-Related Skills

Job-related skills are abilities related to a particular job. For example, an auto mechanic needs to know how to tune an engine and an accountant needs to know how to balance a ledger. You learn these job-related skills in a variety of ways, including through education, training, work, hobbies, or through other life experiences.

Unlike transferable skills, job-related skills may require retooling when it comes time to embark on your "green" career. If the "green" job you're looking at closely resembles jobs you've had in the past, you may only need to add the necessary "green" education, and then do essentially the same type of work for a "green" company. In fact, those skills—coupled with your newly developed green knowledge—will make you a highly prized applicant. A top selling auto sales representative with a little training on hybrid technology will be able to educate customers about the benefits of a hybrid car to the environment and to their own pocketbooks, increasing his company's bottom line.

In some cases, a substantial investment in education and training may be required, however. A public relations specialist moving into a career as an animal rights advocate will have many of the job-related skills she needs already (excellent communication and people skills, for example). That same PR specialist looking to land a job as a hydrologist or a chemical engineer, on the other hand, will need to go back to school, probably for an entirely different degree. Depending on the skills required, your career goals could require more than just a coat of "green" paint on top of what you've already done—it may require a new foundation.

After you can identify what skills you have, you can better match yourself to the kinds of opportunities available to you. In addition, knowing your skills and being able to communicate them effectively will help you in your job search, in interviews, and when retooling your resume. The key is to know what your current skills qualify you for and to match them to your career goals. If they don't match, then you must take the steps required to get the skills you need.

Identify Your Career Goals

How can you tell whether you have skills required for your new career if you're not even sure what career you're seeking? In the last chapter we showed you how to research "green" careers with the hopes that a few would speak to you. But even if you have an idea of the kind of job you want, that's not the same as having a goal.

Identifying a realistic and appropriate green career goal involves assessing

- **Your experience:** Acquired through education, previous employment, volunteer work, and other sources, your experience prepares you to carry out the job responsibilities required in your new green career field.

- **Your strengths:** A career choice should primarily rely upon your strengths. Your weaknesses should never be those skills or aptitudes critical to success in the job.

- **Your personal preferences:** A career choice should allow you to do what you like to do and to perform tasks you do well. It should also meet your goals for lifestyle needs, future opportunities, work schedule, location, and income potential. These are the factors that must be evaluated in terms of their short-term and long-term impact on your career and life. Because few of us are able to satisfy all of our preferences simultaneously, they should be balanced in a satisfactory manner.

- **Your targeted industries and jobs:** In what industries are there markets for your skills? What types of positions do you qualify for in these industries? What distinctive qualifications would you bring to the employer? Answers to these questions are based upon your unique combination of experience, strengths, and preferences. For this reason, they usually require careful consideration.

You already have some idea about your strengths and interests and the type of work environment that fits you best. Now you need to match up what you want and have to offer with what an employer expects. Go back to Chapter 3 and review what you consider to be your strongest skills. Now ask yourself, what kinds of "green" jobs would require those same skills? Take those skills you identified and match them to the kinds of jobs you researched using the resources in Chapter 4 and you are well on your way to having a clear (and attainable) career goal.

> **Painter's Tip:** Counting on your employer to manage your career doesn't work anymore. Job stability and employee loyalty are a thing of the past. Instead you must oversee your own career path and take on a "free agent" mentality. Your career is in your hands.

Know What Employers Want

Job descriptions will list the job-related skills required for the position. Although there are skills specific to each green industry, there are also personal qualities that employers want in just about every job, for example:

- Achievement of organizational objectives

- Achievement of performance standards
- Can-do attitude
- Problem-solving ability
- Flexibility (work schedule, location, duties)
- Previous work experience (evidence that you can do the job)

Think about what you want and then think about what employers prize. Finding the intersection of these two is the key to setting the right career goal and making an effective transition.

EMPLOYERS' TOP TEN

Here's a list of the ten top qualities that employers want, according to Stan Wright, Director at College of the Canyons in Valencia, CA.

- Good communication skills: verbal and written
- Honesty/integrity
- Interpersonal skills (able to relate to others)
- Strong work ethic
- Teamwork
- Analytical/problem-solving skills
- Motivation/initiative
- Flexibility/adaptability
- Computer skills
- Detail oriented

Match Your Preferences to Careers

In the last chapter, you learned about a wealth of resources to help you discover your career options. Hopefully you did some exploring and took notes on some careers that intrigued you. In some cases, these careers might be light years away from what you are doing right now. In other cases, they might represent a horizontal move rather than a dramatic shift. Regardless of the size of the gap between where you are and where you're going, it's time to begin matching some of those possible career choices with your skills and inclinations.

Narrow Down Your Career Choices

Following is a worksheet that you can use to evaluate and focus your green career choices. You can reproduce the page and answer the questions for each career that you are exploring. This should help you to get a clearer picture of which choice would be the best match for you. Be sure to use a separate sheet for each occupation you want to explore.

CAREER EVALUATION WORKSHEET

Occupation: _____

Industry: _____

1. List the skills and abilities required for this occupation:

   _____

   _____

2. List the skills, experience, and education you already have that will prepare you for this occupation (include transferrable skills learned in another occupation):

   _____

   _____

3. List additional skills, experience, and education you need to secure a job in this occupation:

   _____

   _____

4. List your personal strengths that would be beneficial in this occupation:

   _____

   _____

5. List your hobbies and interests related to your occupation:

   _____

   _____

6. List any personal weaknesses that may affect your ability to perform well in this occupation:

_____

_____

7. Is the demand for this occupation growing by more than 10% in your area? Yes/No

8. How much could you expect to earn in this occupation:

$_____

9. Is there opportunity for growth in this field? Yes/No

Career Ladder: from _____ to _____

10. What are the typical hours/ shifts you will need to work?

_____

11. Other important information about this occupation:

_____

_____

_____

Having done the research on job duties, salary expectations, and additional training required for three or four jobs of interest, you now have the information required to evaluate and select your best match and can begin to set goals for yourself.

Painter's Tip: Weigh the pros and cons of your new career direction carefully and see where they balance out. The cost of a two-year college degree may well be worth it if it will double your salary. On the other hand, a job in fuel cell technology may *not* be worth it if it means moving halfway across the country for a job. There will always be tradeoffs—just be sure the positives outweigh the negatives.

Set Your Goals

It's one thing to say you want to change careers; it's another to develop a serious plan that lays out a timeline to complete the steps required.

Look at the following sample goal worksheet and action plan. Note the answers as well as the timeline that follows. Then it will be your turn to create your own.

SAMPLE GOAL WORKSHEET

Identify Your Specific Goal (with completion date if applicable)

I will land a customer service representative or lead sales role with a solid organization selling a green-related product with a salary of $60,000 within 25 miles of my home by September 20, 20xx.

Benefits of Reaching This Goal:

Help the environment by selling a green product

Less worry because now employed in a stable career

Less tension within family

Can meet financial obligations

Obstacles Keeping Me from Reaching This Goal:

Not familiar with the green product (need to learn)

Not a lot of customer relations experience

They might be looking for younger workers

I'm not very organized

I'm worried whether I can stay motivated

Questions I Still Need to Answer:

How does this job make best use of my skills/interests?

How to put together/execute an action plan?

Where are the jobs located?

How to tailor my resumes/cover letters to address this green opportunity?

What do different levels of this job pay?

Resources to Draw Upon in Answering These Questions:

My family

My past coworkers

My community college

List of Internet job sites

Job search books

SAMPLE ACTION PLAN

ACTION STEPS	TARGET DATE
1. Discuss situation with support group (for example, family, friends, coworkers)	7/7
2. Establish budget, timetable for completing action steps	7/9
3. Exercise daily, pace self to keep stress in check	Ongoing
4. Identify suitable financial resources (COBRA, Unemployment, food stamps, and so on)	7/10
5. Visit college career center	7/12
6. Take one or more career assessments and meet with career counselor to discuss results	7/13
7. Review career center event calendars—sign up for job search workshops	7/16

(continued)

(continued)

ACTION STEPS	TARGET DATE
8. Utilize career center and college resources to identify suitable green jobs, research each job on the Internet	Ongoing
9. Talk to people in the green field I am considering and do informational interviews	7/20
10. Attend a conference in the green area I am considering	7/22
11. Review list of temporary help agencies; select/visit two	7/23
12. Review job skills workshop's guidelines on resumes and cover letters	7/23
13. Draft resume template that is easily modifiable	7/24
14. Research comprehensive list of Internet job sites	7/25
15. Identify Internet jobs of interest— apply/keep records	Ongoing
16. Identify local companies; discuss contact strategy with counselor	Ongoing
17. Review job search workshop materials on interview preparation	7/27
18. Explore pay levels for different jobs of interest	7/28
19. Review workshop materials on follow-up letters/thank-you notes	7/30

Now, it's your turn. Use the following worksheets to fill in your own set of goals and the steps you will take to reach them. Keep in mind that the preceding example is a short timetable and does not factor in many of the complexities you might face. For example, you might target a four or five course credential program that could take a year to complete. That time should be included in your action plan.

If your plan includes a period of time when you intend to work and put away money to pay for your career change, then include that time, but set a definite date with a realistic goal, such as "by 11/1/XX I will have $3,500 set aside to pay for courses." With a specific time schedule and money goal it becomes much easier to budget and plan.

GOAL WORKSHEET

Sample Job Search Action Plan

Identify Your Specific Goal (with completion date if applicable)

_____

_____

_____

Benefits of Reaching This Goal:

_____

_____

_____

Obstacles Keeping Me from Reaching This Goal:

_____

_____

_____

_____

Questions I Still Need to Answer:

_____

_____

_____

_____

(continued)

(continued)

Resources to Draw Upon in Answering These Questions:

_____

_____

_____

_____

_____

ACTION PLAN

ACTION STEPS	TARGET DATE
1. _____	_____
_____	_____
2. _____	_____
_____	_____
3. _____	_____
_____	_____
4. _____	_____
_____	_____
5. _____	_____
_____	_____
6. _____	_____
_____	_____

ACTION STEPS	TARGET DATE
7. _____	_____
_____	_____
8. _____	_____
_____	_____
9. _____	_____
_____	_____
10. _____	_____
_____	_____
11. _____	_____
_____	_____
12. _____	_____
_____	_____
13. _____	_____
_____	_____
14. _____	_____
_____	_____
15. _____	_____
_____	_____

In this chapter we have given you exercises to help you define your green career goal and formulate a plan of action with a timeline to achieve this goal. Now that you have a career choice in mind, you need to know how to find jobs in your new field. The next two chapters will help you answer this question.

CHAPTER 6

Finding the Right Opportunity

Let's say that you have chosen your new green occupation and are completing the training you included in your career plan. Now it's time to start investigating job opportunities.

In this chapter, we'll show you where green jobs are advertised. Even better, we'll show you how to narrow down the companies where you would like to work and then figure out how to contact people within those companies in order to be considered for jobs that aren't even advertised. After all, searching for the right job is all about knowing the best place to dig.

Find the Right Company for You

You can't find the right company for you if you don't know what you're looking for. Rather than waiting and hoping to see a job advertisement from a company you would love to work for, you need to take control of your job search and find those companies yourself. That means attending trade shows, researching company websites, and networking with others in the industry. It requires some legwork and a little courage, but it will pay off in opportunities that others don't even know about yet.

Create a Prospective Employer's Profile

It's always easier to grocery shop if you bring the list. The same is true of finding potential employers. You need to know specifically what you want. As you get started, ask yourself these questions:

- Does the company have to be local or are you willing to move?

- If you are not willing to move, how far are you willing to commute? If you drew a circle with your home at the center, how large would the circle be and what cities would be included?

- If you're willing to move, what area are you willing to move to and what region of the country do you want to avoid?

- Do you want to work for a small company, a large one, or either?

- What industry or industries are you targeting? For example, do you specifically want to work for a company within a green industry or are you willing to work in a green *position* for a company *outside* the green industry?

- What kind of company culture fits you? Are you looking for a company where employees work together regardless of department? Are you looking for a company where employees socialize through lots of company-sponsored events?

- Are you looking for a company that offers specific benefits? Do you need a good health plan for your family? Are you looking for a 401(k)?

- Are you more comfortable working for a large company where roles are clearly defined or a small company?

- Does the company promote aggressively from within? Is growth potential an important consideration for you?

After you've answered these questions, you will know how large the universe of potential employers is for you and where to start looking for the right company.

KEEPING TRACK OF YOUR PROGRESS

Keeping track of your job search is a conscious, daily effort. Be sure to debrief yourself after any networking event while the information is still fresh in your mind. For each contact you make, write down at least the following information (in addition to the information on the business card):

- Where did you meet this person?

- What did you discuss?

- Did the person give you a referral? If so, include that information.

- Is there any follow-up you both agreed on?

Keep this information in a notebook, spreadsheet, database, or some other contact management software.

Being a Trade Show Detective

One way to learn about a lot of companies in a very short period of time and gather a lot of potential contacts is to go to a trade show for the industry you would like to work in. Let's say that you wanted to work for the solar energy industry; then you would do well to attend the Solar Power International (SPI) tradeshow sponsored by the Solar Energy Industries Association and the Solar Electric Power Association. Such conferences are a goldmine of information for anyone looking to become part of the solar industry.

Hundreds of companies attend these events to showcase their green innovations in every aspect of the economy. The job opportunities represented at the 2010 conference, for example, included component manufacturers and system manufacturers, retail companies selling products to the public, services companies that focus on installation and support, and supply chain personnel including distributors and integrators. In short, these trade shows are not just for scientists with advanced degrees—they are for anyone interested in the industry.

Trade shows and conferences provide excellent opportunities to network and learn about companies as well as about the industry you're pursuing. Most conferences include networking events such as receptions and luncheons—perfect for sniffing out job opportunities and swapping business cards. In addition, conferences such as SPI also feature speakers and presenters who might be excellent contacts to make.

> **Painter's Tip:** Most trade shows like SPI include an "exhibit hall only" option and a student option when registering. These options cost far less than the normal registration fee. Look into them.

If you attend a trade show or conference, make a list of the companies you want to visit and prioritize it. Keep in mind that the salespeople in the exhibit have far different priorities than you do. They want to talk with potential customers first. So, wait until the traffic thins at an exhibit before striking up a conversation. When networking at a conference or other large event, be sure to do the following:

- Ask for a business card.

- Ask about hiring policies. Is it done at the departmental level? Do you have to go through HR?

- Inquire about the manager in the department you are interested in. Get a name and number or e-mail if possible.

- Ask what the company's latest product initiatives are. It's likely to be exhibited so ask for a demo. Be sure to take notes.

- Ask what the company's major competitive advantages are. Also ask who the salesperson considers to be the leading competitors.

- Ask what the salesperson likes most about working for the company.

- Respect the exhibitor's time.

Painter's Tip: Strike up conversations with attendees wherever you find them—at lunch, on the bus, in the hall. You should walk away with a couple of dozen new contacts and some notes about a number of companies. If you do a trade show the right way, you should be totally exhausted from walking, talking, and networking by the end of the day.

Treat trade shows as social networking opportunities. Set a goal for yourself and see how many contacts you can make, not just with exhibitors, but with everyone in attendance. Here are some questions to keep in mind when you're talking with attendees:

- Do they know whether their own company is hiring? If so, is there someone you could contact?

- How did they go about getting their job? Are there any tricks and tips they could share?

- Do they know of any *other* company that might be hiring?

- Is there anyone else from their company at the trade show who you could meet who might be able to fill you in on the industry and opportunities for employment?

You might only be able to ask a couple of these questions, but every nugget of information you can gather is valuable. Remember that people who attend professional trade shows are generally far more influential and dedicated than those who don't.

In addition to all the great contacts you can make, most trade shows have a job center where you can look over the latest job openings and apply for positions. That means you should bring some resumes with you. Keep in mind, though, that trade shows generally attract people with a lot of experience in the industry, so the jobs being advertised might require far more experience than you have.

Finding a Trade Show in Your Chosen Industry

There are a number of ways to find out about trade shows in the industry or industries you've targeted. Here are our favorites:

- Google the key phrase for your industry and "trade show." For example, typing "wind energy" and "trade show" into Google results in at least 30 different trade show listings.

- Go to the website of a leading company in the industry you've targeted. Many companies will list the trade shows where they exhibit.

- Go to a news website for the industry you've targeted. As an example, we went to the Renewable Energy World.com website (www.renewableenergyworld.com) and typed "trade show" into the website's search engine. The result was a large listing of various trade shows in the area of renewable energy.

Using Professional Associations to Harvest Company Contacts

Reputable companies spend lots of money to become part of professional and trade associations. Take solar energy, for example. The Solar Energy Industries Association (www.sei.org) has a directory of member companies. This directory allows you to search for companies by state as well as by other key terms. So if you've decided that your job search should be restricted to companies within a certain geographical area, this type of professional association member directory is an excellent place to start.

You might even find companies listed in categories you hadn't even considered as tied to a particular industry. The day we happened to examine the Electric Drive Transportation Association list, we found companies and organizations categorized as follows:

- Automotive and Other Vehicle Manufacturers
- Energy Companies
- Battery and Battery Component Manufacturers

- Component Suppliers
- Infrastructure Developers
- Industry Trade Associations
- Universities
- Government Organizations
- Multi-Industry Organizations
- Defense Contractors

Maybe you hadn't thought of working for a defense contractor, but tanks and ships can be energy efficient, too. Note that member companies and organizations are listed with a link to their own website, so it's easy to gather additional information. While you are on the website of a professional association, be sure to look for press releases generally grouped under the "News" category. These press releases describe important trends in the industry and often contain quotes from people in the member companies. You can add these names and company affiliations to your growing database of possible contacts. In Chapter 7 you will learn how to use social networking tools such as LinkedIn, Facebook, and Twitter to communicate with them.

Researching the Companies Themselves

Let's assume you've built up a list of possible employers. The next step is to research these companies in a very systematic way. As you will see, a lot of elements within a company's website are worth examining.

The "About" Section

Virtually every company website has an "About" section where you can learn more about the company. Often these sections contain the company's mission statement, the scope of its business, its major products or services, the size of its operation, and its future plans. This can be a great resource for deciding whether a company is a good fit for you. Does it seem to match your values? Does it appear to be growing? Is it the right size? In addition, knowing a company's overall mission and philosophy can be especially beneficial if you end up interviewing with it.

The "Careers" Section

The careers section may be called "careers" or "employment" or "human resources." Regardless of the title, this is a must stop in your company research. The careers section usually includes information on company benefits, company culture, hiring practices, and current opportunities. You can use this information to do the following:

- Determine whether you would fit into such an environment.

- Record the benefit information in your growing company database information and later compare it with what other companies offer.

- Learn about actual job titles in the industry as well as what kind of experience is required. You can use that information to help you in modifying your career goals.

- Study the types of jobs being advertised to make some intelligent guesses about which direction the company is headed. Let's say you notice that the company is hiring engineers with Wi-Fi experience. That might indicate that it is planning to create wireless versions of its products.

As you look over a company's posted openings, be sure to look at the general job requirements to see what transferrable skills are valued. Even if you are still finishing up your training and not yet ready to apply for a job, you can study the job description to note where you might be able to use what you learned in a different career to help you qualify. Job descriptions in a career section of a company website are full of valuable information that is well worth studying whether you are ready to apply for the positions or not (and if you are, don't let anything stop you—though you might want to read the rest of this book first).

The "Membership" Section

Many companies list the organizations and associations they are members of. Such lists are worth studying for many reasons. First of all, there will usually be some professional organizations for you to research to find even more potential employers. Second, these organizations usually sponsor trade shows and conferences—and we've already discussed how valuable those can be as sources of contacts and job leads.

The "News" Section

Virtually every company website has a "News" section. Generally you'll find a company's press releases here, but sometimes the section also includes what the press is reporting about the company. In any event, it is a treasure trove of information. You should take some notes on what the company's major initiatives and new product releases are. The press articles will generally include some indication of not only what the company is doing well, but also areas where the company can improve. Once again, this is great background material to help you write a cover letter or formulate questions for an interview.

The "Investor Relations" Section

Public companies always have a section for investors. There you can find the company's annual report as well as its financial disclosures. The company's annual report highlights its strategies and goals as well as lists new initiatives. It also shows how well the company is doing.

You don't have to be an accountant to see whether the company is profitable or not. If the company has had some layoffs, then that is also something to consider when deciding whether it should remain on your list of prospective employers.

THE KEYWORD SEARCH

Many companies screen their applications and resumes electronically looking for certain keywords. That's where reviewing a company's website comes in handy. Using what you glean from their press releases, job descriptions, and product offerings, you can pick out words and phrases that have obvious significance and incorporate them into your resume, application, and cover letter. Doing so will give you an edge over applicants who haven't bothered to do their research.

Trade shows, professional associations, and company websites are all valuable resources for information on specific companies and job opportunities, but they aren't the only ones. You might be surprised how many opportunities you can dig up, just be asking around. In fact, as you'll soon see, that's the best way to find a job.

Networking—the Old-Fashioned Way

In Chapter 7 we will explain how to use social networking sites on the Internet to grow your list of contacts, but you should never neglect the traditional way of networking: through good old-fashioned face time. After all, it has been proven that the very best way to get a job is to network. Employers would rather hire someone who was referred to them than someone who answered an ad in the paper or submitted a resume through Monster. Your contacts are your key to breaking into your green career.

Your network consists of *anyone* who might possibly help you find a job. Let's say that you've just completed your certificate training and now you're researching prospective employers. You need to let people know that you're looking for work so that they can spread the word. You might start with the following:

- Teachers in your certificate program

- Friends and relatives

- The fraternity or sorority members you still contact

- Former colleagues

- And anyone, no matter how casually you're acquainted, who happens to ask what's new in your life

What you are looking for is for someone to mention that they know someone who is working in your chosen industry, maybe even a company that you are interested in. If they do, ask them to help introduce you to that person. Make it clear that at this point you are just looking for help in learning about the company and the industry.

When you talk with the person, explain what your goal is and what your training consists of, and then start asking them questions about the industry and the company where they work. If the conversation goes well and the person is friendly, you might ask whether there is anyone else they can recommend that you talk to.

As your contact list grows, your knowledge of the company and other companies in the industry also will grow. If you are ready to begin applying for positions, you can ask about the hiring process. Explain the type of position you are seeking and ask who heads up that area within the company. Remember: It's always better to have a departmental contact than to go through the HR department.

Painter's Tip: You might ask your contact whether it's okay to use his or her name when applying. Many companies give a bonus to employees who recommend someone who later is hired. An insider's name mentioned early in a cover letter will likely cause your application to receive more attention.

Although the best way to find career opportunities is to ask around, it doesn't hurt to make direct contact with those who you know share your interests or are already part of the industry. The rest of this chapter looks at a few more ways you can make contact with employers and others in your industry. Just remember that the more contacts you make, the easier it will be for you to find the kind of position you want.

Attending Green Job Fairs

If you Google "green job fairs," you will find a number of listings in virtually all states. Unlike trade fairs or conferences, job fairs attract companies that are definitely hiring, so bring resumes with you. The nice thing about job fairs is that the companies are usually local or at least close regionally. They attend because they have openings and they are shopping around for qualified candidates.

Painter's Tip: Be warned: A number of entrepreneurs use job fairs to hook people into working for them in their get-rich-quick schemes. Don't pay attention to any multi-level marketing ploy or any scheme where you have to lay out money for a franchise.

Although employers are the primary draw, don't forget to talk with other attendees. You will be amazed at the kind of information you can glean from people who have been in the green job market, particularly if you are not searching for the same type of job. Finally, don't be surprised if you are interviewed right there on the spot—it has happened before. Come to the job fair ready to make your sales pitch and a great first impression. For more information on where to find green job fairs, go to www.greenjobs. net/green-job-fairs.

Joining Professional Organizations

As we mentioned earlier in the chapter, just about every industry has one or more professional organizations associated with it, and joining these can

105

be well worth the time and money in dues. These organizations offer local meetings as well as volunteer opportunities at which you can meet people working in your targeted industry. They can become part of your network that will help you learn about specific companies and steer you toward job opportunities.

Painter's Tip: A perfect time to join a professional association is when you are still in an education or training program as most of these organizations have special student rates.

Consider the American Water Works Association (www.awwa.org), for example. The AWWA website points to an annual convention that recently hosted 11,600 water professionals. Clearly this trade show offers enormous opportunity for you to meet representatives from a number of water companies. Equally important, the national organization has local section meetings that you can attend to meet water professionals in your own hometown.

Professional organizations also give you the opportunity to solve real environmental problems through volunteering. This gives you valuable hands-on experience as well as additional chances to rub shoulders with professionals already in the field. The American Water Works Association, for example, has more than 250 volunteer units that provide opportunities for service.

In addition, joining a professional association provides you with a wealth of technical material about your profession that often is difficult to obtain unless you already work for a company in that industry. The awwa.org website contains a large Professional and Technical Resources section with technical manuals, standards, and even discussion groups where you can discuss water problems. The section also contains a Career Center page that offers career advice as well as the ability to search through current job openings, as well as information on various water certifications and how to obtain them.

Painter's Tip: Virtually all professional organizations include journals and newsletters as part of a membership. These materials are valuable for helping you fill in any gaps in you education as well as provide you with good material to prepare for job interviews.

Chapter 11 lists a number of organizations specifically designed for environmental professionals looking for like-minded people. If in doubt, use the URLs to visit the organizations' websites and study them. Ask your instructors which organizations they recommend, and then go join one!

Becoming Active in an Environmental Group

We're hoping that you have targeted a green career goal not just because green jobs are on the upswing, but also because you really believe in sustainability. Many green companies specifically indicate in their job descriptions that they are looking for like-minded people who also want to make the world greener. One way to establish your interest in improving the environment is to volunteer.

Besides the obvious benefit of establishing your green credibility, there are other advantages to volunteering. You will feel good about doing something to improve the world. You will also meet a lot of interesting, committed people who will increase your network of contacts and knowledge of green companies. It's a win/win situation. One quick way to find volunteer opportunities is to go to the One Earth One Mission website (www.oeom. org), which, at last glance, contained more than 60 different volunteering opportunities with various environmental groups.

If your volunteering goal is to become an activist, then the perfect place for you to go online is Activists Wanted.org. In addition, Chapter 11 contains URLs for a number of environmental organizations. In some cases they are umbrella organizations that consolidate volunteer opportunities across a wide spectrum of groups.

Here are some questions you should ask yourself as you look through the volunteer opportunities:

- Does the group match your level of activism? Some groups push the boundaries when it comes to confronting companies and government officials. So, read what the group does and make sure it matches up with your comfort zone. Also remember that future employers will associate you with whatever volunteer organizations you join.

- Does the group allow you to volunteer for activities that closely align with your career goals? In other words, if you are interested in becoming a water sustainability professional, can you actually work on a water project?

- Do you want to work on local issues or national and global environmental issues? Check to see if the group's scope matches your own.

- How many different volunteer activities are offered? Take the Sierra Club as an example. Not only do you have the opportunity to take action by supporting various environmental issues via e-mail to your senators and representatives, but you also can even take any one of 90 different volunteer service vacations that the club's website describes as ranging from "helping with research projects at whale calving grounds in Maui to assisting with archaeological site restoration in New Mexico."

- Are you looking for a family volunteering experience? Some organizations offer activities for the entire family. These organizations make it possible to help your children grow up environmentally aware.

Regardless of the kind of volunteering you do, make sure that experience finds its way on your resume, in your application, or in your portfolio. Especially as green jobs are concerned, volunteering is not just a good way to learn new skills, it also showcases your values and your dedication—two things an employer will be happy to see.

Looking at Green Job Boards

The very best way to find a green job is to research companies, talk with individuals, locate key contacts, and actively look to *create* an opening for yourself. After all, after a job is publicly listed, your odds as a career changer to match up perfectly with it are relatively low. It's much easier to fit a mold when you have helped create the shape rather than hope the mold fits you.

Still, it is possible that you might find a job advertised where your transferrable skills match up very closely with the requirements, and that's why green job boards can be useful. Chapter 11 provides a list of some of the more popular green job boards. Keep in mind that most green professional associations also have their own job boards as well.

While it is worth the effort to apply for a job on a job board if you match up very closely, there are other major advantages of studying job boards, including the following:

- **Learn the lingo.** Every industry has its own jargon and its own job titles. Learning this language will help you refine your resume and answer interview questions.

- **Learn the names of companies in green industries.** Go from the job boards to the employer's website and study it. If the company looks interesting, add it to your list of possible employers.

- **Learn the experience and training requirements for different levels of the position you are targeting.** In other words, if you learn what type of position requires 5 years of experience and what type of position requires 10 years of experience, you can revise your career plan accordingly. Then, when you have your interview, you will be able to talk about your long-range as well as your short-term career goals.

Start Looking

This chapter has shown you how to really dig up information about companies and the kinds of opportunities they offer. The key point we want to make is that you should not passively wait for the right green career opportunity to suddenly appear. Instead, you should systematically research specific green companies and contact the ones you are most interested in. By the time you are ready to interview with a company, you should know enough about it to make it abundantly clear to an interviewer that you would be an immediate contributor and an asset to that company.

Making contact with the right people isn't always easy. You might not be able to fly to every trade show or attend every conference. Companies may be reluctant to talk to total strangers who have tracked them down through press releases. Networking takes time and energy. In the next chapter, we will show you how to make it easier, at least, by leveraging the technology offered through social media.

CHAPTER 7

Social Networking

Imagine sitting at lunch with a colleague who mentions a friend of his. "Bill's an old fraternity buddy. You should meet him because he works for a company that could use someone like you." It may sound too good to be true, but it happens more often than you think.

Social networking takes place every time you meet some friends and they take the opportunity to introduce you to someone they know. People have been growing and mining their social networks for opportunities for years. Realtors, for example, automatically ask everyone they meet if they happen to know anyone who is looking to buy or sell a house. Your neighborhood insurance agent probably routinely asks you whether you know of any friends who might need insurance.

Whenever you meet new people, they will inevitably ask what you do for a living. When you tell them about your new career aspirations and ask whether they know anyone you could talk to, *that's* social networking in practice.

You're Closer Than You Realize

Several years ago, the movie *Six Degrees of Separation* created buzz with the concept that everyone is connected to virtually everyone else via six or fewer contacts. Think of someone completely out of your social set. You might not know Donald Trump, for example. You might find to your surprise that your brother-in-law went to school with a friend whose sister had a roommate in college who knew the nanny for one of Donald Trump's children. If you're only a few contacts separated from Donald Trump, imagine how much more plausible it is that you are only a few contacts separated from a key department head for a company with a green focus.

Statistics show that the people you know (or can meet) provide access to 70% of the job market no matter what type of job you are looking for.

What that means is the more people you talk to, the better your chance of getting a job! Social networking to find a job in a green industry is even more necessary, because many of those jobs are just now emerging and your immediate circle of friends might not know anyone working for a green company. Still, nobody will help you if they don't know you *want* their help, so you start be telling people who you are and what you are looking for.

> **Painter's Tip:** Finding the right job is often a matter of being in the right place at the right time. But if you do it right, *you* pick the place and time. Some call it luck, others just call it hard work.

But who should you talk to? Of course your first contacts are your family and friends. Don't be afraid. There is no longer a stigma associated with being unemployed or thinking about an entirely new career. Tell your family and friends because *they* have family and friends and the ground you can cover expands exponentially.

Some other people who could be part of your job-hunting network include

- **Old friends from work.** They will hear of opportunities that you don't. You may have friends landing new jobs of their own. As they get secure in their position, they can recommend you to their new company.

- **Teachers and instructors.** They will often know about job openings in your field or can let you know about upcoming job fairs. If you take classes in green technology, for example, the instructors are likely to already be well-placed in that field. Even if their companies do not have job openings, they might know colleagues doing similar work for other companies.

- **Acquaintances at your place of worship, neighbors, or former military buddies.** These people are all inclined to help one another with job hunting. Look through your e-mail address book or holiday card mailing list and you'll find many people worth talking to. You can also ask people at your gym, your child's sports team, or any other recreational gathering.

- **Professionals who see a lot of people in their line of work.** Doctors, dentists, hairdressers, manicurists, tax advisors—they have contact with a wide variety of people. There's a good chance they know someone who might help you.

How to Network Successfully

When it comes to networking with your family and friends, you simply ask for their help. Make it clear that you're interested in not only finding a job in your new career field but in anything that might *lead* to a job.

With people you know less well, bring up your job search in the course of a conversation. Say, "I'd appreciate it if you'd keep me in mind," or "Let me know if you hear of anything." Then give them your business card or resume so they can do just that.

Remember the people you ask at the start probably won't know of any openings or opportunities. That's why you ask all of your contacts if they *know* of someone who could help you with your search.

> **Painter's Tip:** Be sure to carry a good supply of business cards with you at all times and give one to every potential contact, because you never know when you might meet someone. Business cards can be made easily and inexpensively at www.vistaprint.com.

GET OUT OF YOUR COMFORT ZONE

Some people spend a lot of time talking about looking for work and not enough time actually looking for work. Talking to your brother or close friend about how hard it is to find a job can be a good way to vent your frustration and get much-needed emotional support, but it can also keep you from doing the hard work of building your network and finding job leads.

People you are close to can be counted on for a lot, but they won't always know of opportunities. You have to be willing to expand your network—contacting people you don't know as well, and then contacting people they know that you might have never met before. It can seem a little daunting at first, but it is the surest way to find a job.

You never know when the perfect connection will arise. Here's a true story. A friend of ours, who we'll call James, took the train to work every day. Over time he got to know a few of his fellow passengers reasonably well. One day he told one of these new friends that his boss had just given him notice that he was going to be laid off. He dreaded telling his wife. The traveling companion mentioned that there was a new opening at his company. He offered to refer James to his boss. Sure enough, that boss decided to interview James later that same day and hired him by Friday of that week.

The reason social networking is so important today is because companies are overwhelmed with job applicants and resumes. In many cases, they simply use software to filter applications. The odds of making it through a pile of resumes and reaching the attention of a hiring manager are only slightly better than the chances of winning the lottery. Don't fight the slush pile; avoid it by getting recommended to the people who have the authority to hire you. They aren't that many degrees away.

> **Painter's Tip:** Keep in mind that the job of human resources or a personnel department is to screen *out* job candidates. It is usually the department managers or the owners of the companies (if the companies are small enough) who get the final say on who to let *in*.

Asking for help isn't difficult, but it can be time consuming if you're not asking the right people. For example, how many of your relatives have even heard about green sustainability, let alone know someone working for a company in this emerging field? Add your relatives' friends and the odds increase, but it would still help if you had access to people who were already in the loop. Thankfully, we live in an age where the whole world is just a tweet away.

GET INVOLVED

As you prepare for a green career, you are likely to find certain environmental issues that resonate with you. It might be safeguarding our water; using wind, geothermal, or solar power to reduce our oil dependence; slowing global warming; protecting wildlife; or any one of a hundred other causes.

As we mentioned in the previous chapter, there are countless green organizations that can provide you with educational materials as well as local meetings where you can rub elbows with like-minded folks. The Sierra Club, the Nature Conservancy, and the Clean Water Network are examples of organizations where you can learn about green jobs as well as get to know others who share your interests.

How do you find the right organization for you? A simple Google search of environmental organizations and your particular state or city often will result in dozens of entries. You'll also find lots of help locating major environmental groups in Chapter 11.

Using Social Networking Sites

While logging face time with your contacts is still one of the most effective ways to find a job, it's not always the fastest or most efficient. In fact, the most effective approach to social networking is to use that traditional approach *and* the Internet. Electronic social networking tools can be especially valuable when pursuing a green career because you can cast a wider net to find people in this relatively new sector of the economy.

In addition to meeting new people, social networking sites make it easy to reconnect with people you've known in the past. With these sites in mind, we can broaden the list of possible contacts that we suggested earlier in this chapter. Your list of people who could possibly serve as contacts that help you launch your green career could include many of the following, even if you've lost touch with them:

- Colleagues from previous jobs
- Classmates from college and/or high school
- Customers from previous jobs
- People who worked for competitors
- Fraternity brothers or sorority sisters
- Ex-bosses
- Distant relatives
- Professional acquaintances you've met at various trade shows and conventions
- College professors
- People you met at various social events

Because social networking sites are so widespread and easy to use, they are fast becoming *the* way to keep in touch with your contacts. Here are couple of other reasons you should begin networking online as soon as possible:

- Just as it takes a while to build relationships with people you see on the job, it takes time to build an electronic social network to the point where it really becomes an effective career tool. You can't do it too quickly or people will be offended by what they feel is an attempt to use them without providing them with any value in return.

Meeting people electronically and asking them immediately for help in finding a key contact or even for a reference is like meeting a complete stranger for the first time and asking for a loan.

- With some social networking tools such as a blog—a website where you offer your views on various subjects—it takes time for people to discover you and to begin coming to your site on a regular basis. The same is true when it comes to using Twitter. You need to build your reputation first.

Electronic social networking should be part of your overall career plan and should be started the moment you set your goals. The more you keep at, the more contacts you will make, and the greater your chances of finding the right job when you are ready.

Of course with an estimated two billion users, the Internet is vast. There are hundreds of ways to network online, but we will just cover the most common and show how you can use each to help you break in to your new green career.

Facebook

If you're not already using Facebook (www.facebook.com), you've probably at least heard about it. This website represents the world's largest electronic social network. While it began as a social site, an increasing number of businesses are now using it for marketing and networking purposes. You could paint your career green without a Facebook account, of course, but you would be missing out on the opportunity to connect to more than 500 million people—one of which surely has a job for you.

To get started, you need to establish a Facebook page (if you don't have one already). After you plug in some basic information, you can begin using the site to locate people; however, there are some conventions you need to follow. For starters, it's awkward to ask complete strangers to be your "friend." If there is a person you think you used to know, write him a note and ask him whether he is the same person who spilled punch on you while you were dancing at a party back at "Raccoon High" or "Polymorph U." If he is the same person, it's likely he'll be happy to "friend" you, upping your list of contacts.

CULTIVATE YOUR (DIGITAL) IMAGE

One of the worst things you can do is to get carried away with your Facebook page and display pictures or post comments that might offend a future boss. A picture of you dancing shirtless with a lampshade on your head might be funny, but it's not something that you want to share with the world. Don't get carried away and let your friends write graffiti on the walls of your Facebook page either, as you may be judged by the friends you have and what they say.

Your digital persona is your responsibility. Keep it clean and professional. Make sure you know about any personal information out in the ether, and don't post anything that might make a bad impression later.

After you have a Facebook page and a reasonable number of friends, it's worth letting them know about your new career aspirations. Keep them up to date on how your classes are coming. The highest percentage of job referrals resulting in actual job *offers* comes not from your closest friends, but from far more distant relationships. One of your "friends" might be talking to someone who in turn knows someone who might work for a company who needs good people.

Using Facebook to Reach Companies

Many companies have begun to sponsor Facebook pages of their own. Smartsynch is an example of a small smart grid company with a Facebook presence. It's very valuable for you to become a Facebook fan of green companies in a field you're interested in joining. You can learn all kinds of information, including but not limited to

- The company's major initiatives.
- The hobbies of people who represent the company.
- The names of key people at the company who blog.
- Common complaints of that company's customers.
- Specialized positions the company is hiring for.
- Events the company is sponsoring or hosting, such as conferences or job fairs.

If you're not sure what companies to follow on Facebook, you can begin by becoming a fan of Facebook sites that will point you to key companies. If you are interested in smart grid technology, as an example, you can become a fan of *smartgridnews* and receive alerts whenever that site publishes a new article on the topic.

Becoming a Fan of Green Organizations

Becoming a fan of a number of green organizations on Facebook is easy. If you're interested in geothermal energy, for example, there's *Geothermania*. If you want to receive updates on a variety of green topics, become a fan of *The Daily Green (TDG)*. Other notable groups worth becoming fans of include *Chelsea Green Publishing*, which offers a broad assortment of information on the politics and practice of sustainable living, and *Sustainable Industries Magazine*, which provides great information on potential employers as well as the names of key contacts already in the industry. Becoming a fan of *Green Festival* will keep you up to date not only on green festivals but also on green businesses.

If you really plan to have a green career, you need to learn to speak the language and understand the key issues, whether technical, political, or social. The best way to get up to speed is to receive green news on a variety of subjects daily and immerse yourself in the content. When content changes on a site where you're a fan, you'll be notified so you can read it.

Think of the information you absorb daily from your Facebook news feeds as well as news feeds from other green websites as multivitamins that are strengthening you, smartening you up, and making you someone a company would be happy to hire.

Broadening Your Contacts on Facebook

Imagine Facebook as a huge room full of people (500 million people—it's a *really* big room) who are engaged in hundreds of thousands of simultaneous conversations. It's daunting when you first walk in. Linger and enjoy the view. If you have something to add, do so, but consider how you want people to think of you.

The groups we've mentioned so far are just a taste of the many green groups you'll find on Facebook. Use the search function in Facebook to locate specific ones. More and more professional groups are joining every day, and it's likely there are groups related to your new career. Go to these group pages and explore. Note the group's interests and the types of comments fans write. Look at who contributes. You can add your own comments, or you can contact some of these people to have a private conversation. Just be completely up front about what you are doing. Make it clear that you're in the process of changing your career and you're interested in some inside information or advice. Most people are willing to help if you are polite, honest, and sincere.

Don't bombard someone with questions; instead try to focus on a couple of key concerns you have. You don't want to be a pest, but you do want to gather some valuable information and begin the process of developing enough of a relationship so that this person becomes a supporter of your career change.

Establishing Your Presence

Social networking is a two-way street. The people you've contacted will, in turn, check out your Facebook page and keep up with your career change. One way to make *your* Facebook page even more helpful in your career planning is to include links that help people appreciate your skills. You could have a link to a blog where you comment regularly on green topics that interest you. You also could have a link to some career-related materials you're particularly proud of. If you gave a talk at a conference, you could have a link to the streaming video file. In other words, think of your Facebook page as a gigantic bulletin board on which you can paste materials that present you in the best light.

VIDEO RESUME PROS AND CONS

Some people go a bit overboard with their self-marketing and include video resumes on their Facebook pages. While this does get your face in front of employers (literally), it also has its pitfalls.

People have strange prejudices that are difficult to imagine. Does your hairstyle remind the potential interviewer of someone he dated who rejected him? Is there a picture in the background that some interviewers consider to be in terrible taste? The whole point of a resume is to get an interview in person. When you actually are sitting down with someone face to face, you have a chance to come across positively despite appearances. If your video resume turns off potential interviewers, you've already lost that chance.

LinkedIn

No social networking site is more useful when it comes to helping you find people who can help you with your new career than LinkedIn. It is a site designed for networking in the traditional, business sense. Think of Facebook as that weekend party with friends and acquaintances, and LinkedIn is a business luncheon—a little more career-focused, if not *quite* as popular.

You begin by creating your own profile that is a resume of sorts—jobs you've held and places you've worked. It's worthwhile spending some time making the profile as complete as possible because for many people, this profile becomes their resume. You can even use links at other social networking websites, such as Facebook, to point back to your LinkedIn profile.

Painters Tip: It is a good idea to add a term such as "green," "environmental," "eco," or "sustainability" to your resume because Google searches include LinkedIn profiles and including these terms will help direct other green-oriented people to your profile.

Just as with traditional face-to-face networking, the power of LinkedIn lies in the ability of your contacts to refer you to others. Ask some friends and colleagues on LinkedIn to recommend you. Their brief recommendation comments appear on your LinkedIn page and help differentiate you from other career changers. How many recommendations should you get? One good rule is one for every company where you've spent some time.

You should also ask people on LinkedIn to link to you. One way to make this process more efficient is to import your address books from Outlook, Gmail, Yahoo! Mail, or any other mail services you might use. You can do the equivalent of a mass mailing to each person asking if they would like to connect with you. Generally you shouldn't have any problems getting colleagues and anyone who knows you and already is a member of LinkedIn to share their networks. Keep in mind that when people link with you, you can see all of their connections and they can see all yours. As you learned in the last chapter, more connections means more opportunities.

The power of LinkedIn is that every person you link to means that you are now linked to *that* person's network. Where this becomes really important is when you identify a key person or company that you would like to contact. LinkedIn allows you to identify that person, and then it will list how you are connected to that person or that company.

In some cases, it's a second-degree contact (you're connected via someone directly linked to you that is directly connected to that person). It could be an even more distant connection. LinkedIn will ask you whether you would like to request an introduction from the person you know who knows the person you're trying to meet.

Just imagine that you are in the position of being able to launch your new career. You've identified some key people with companies you'd love to work for. After you've typed in the names of these people, LinkedIn will navigate through its database and determine the specific person you know that can help you reach a key decision maker. We don't think there's ever been a more efficient way of reaching the right person.

Using Groups to Broaden Your Network

There's a search function in LinkedIn to help you find people. You can also browse through the list of members from specific companies. LinkedIn will automatically take the list of companies you've worked for and generate a list of people who work or have worked for those companies and ask you if you want to connect with them. There are active university alumni groups and even groups that represent alumni from particular companies as well.

There are hundreds of groups in LinkedIn. At the time we wrote this chapter there were a dozen different subgroups on various aspects of green technology such as

- Clean Tech
- Energy Industry Expertise
- Green Advertising and Marketing
- Green Business Professionals
- Green Energy
- Green Entrepreneurs and Investors

- Green HR
- Green IT Professionals
- Green Jobs and Careers
- Green Publishing
- Sustainability
- Sustainability Professionals

The great thing about these groups is that you can join them for free and take as active a part as you would like. Every time someone in a group posts something, you'll be notified via e-mail. Do you have questions you'd love answered before your interview? You can pose them to the group (provided your interviewer isn't a member). The same applies to any questions about a new technology on the horizon or where the best jobs can be found. It's like attending a trade show but far more efficient.

Equally important, you can contribute answers to questions people pose. In some cases you might have picked up the answer while taking classes or in conducting informational interviews. In any case, you can establish yourself as a helpful person who adds value to the group. After a while it's likely that members of the group might contact you and arrange for a private conversation. It's social networking without the cocktails or valet parking, and unless you're in a webcam-enabled conference call, pajamas are perfectly acceptable.

> **Painter's Tip:** LinkedIn also offers its own listing of jobs, but that's not it's real strength. Keep in mind that while the service is free, there is a fee (now around $25 per month) to upgrade and be able to contact people who are not directly linked to your specific network. For someone ready to look for a new job in a new career field, it might be money well spent.

Twitter

The latest social networking tool available is Twitter. It's a free service where you create a profile and then send out very short messages called "tweets." People can subscribe to your tweets and receive them whenever you send them. In turn, after you have created a profile, you can subscribe to receive other people's tweets.

Why bother? The idea of subscribing to someone else's random thoughts might seem like a waste of time, and it's is true that some people tweet on everything that happens to them no matter how unimportant. Who cares if the person stopped at the market and bought a box of laundry detergent? There are people who spend a good portion of their lives chronicling the minutiae of the moment. On the other hand, the movers and shakers in green industries, as well as virtually all other industries, are also tweeting, and what *they* have to say can be very informative.

Let's take one example. Earth2Tech provides up-to-date information on the latest clean energy companies. One of its leading bloggers is Katie Feherenbacher (katiefehren). More than 2,000 people follow her tweets. By subscribing to her tweets, you can learn about green companies that are unknown to most people. As an example, one of her recent tweets provided a link to her Earth2Tech article that described three stealth solar startups including information on these companies, their funding, their technology, and even key contacts. Armed with that information, you could mount a campaign to be hired even though the company has not even finalized its hiring plans.

There are some specific ways to use Twitter to become a part of the green community. Twestivals are festivals that make use of Twitter to highlight a particular green issue. For example, a group of people who wanted to get a well dug in Africa created a twestival to highlight this issue. Enough people began following the tweets and responding to requests for help that the goal was achieved.

You can easily search Twitter for green-related content. Search "hashtags" such as #green, #eco, and #environment. If you go to Twitter and type in one of these hashtags, you'll see a long listing of tweets from individuals whose content fits under this specific topic.

As an example, when we typed in #environment, we found a tweet by Tom DeRosa who lives in Farmington, Connecticut. It turns out that Tom heads up an executive search company specializing in placing people in the clean energy field. Not only could you follow someone like Tom—who has interesting things to say about clean energy, smart grids, and renewable energy—but his tweets often reference the 67 other people whose tweets *he* is receiving. People who tweet regularly will provide links to other people's tweets as well as their websites. The result is that by following a few key green folks who tweet regularly, you'll suddenly learn about dozens, if not *hundreds* of other interesting people active in green pursuits and have a way to communicate directly with these people.

Tweet Your Brand

While you should certainly use Twitter to expand your list of contacts and unearth green opportunities, you should also use it to enhance our own marketability. Through your tweets you create a "brand" for yourself. In other words, people will soon have an image in their mind of who you are. Ideally they will begin to think of you as someone interested in the key issues associated with your new career and, equally important, someone who has something valuable to say. If you have begun receiving tweets from a number of people active in the green community, you'll find you have lots of interesting topics to discuss.

Painter's Tip: Don't feel that you have to tweet all the time. It gets ridiculous when tweeting becomes an end in itself. Recently a couple was photographed immediately after their wedding ceremony, tweeting away rather than enjoying the moment. You should stick to business-related matters if you want social networking tools to help you with your career objective.

The real value of Twitter is that everything takes place in real time. If something very important in your field is taking place, someone well connected in the industry is likely to tweet about it and give you a link to a video feed so you can view the event as it happens. Some companies even allow job seekers to sign up for instant tweets whenever a position becomes available.

Of course, as we stress over and over again in this book, your best job prospects are those that you learn about that are not publicly listed. So, if someone you follow tweets that the company will be expanding, you might be able to arrange for someone in that company to put in a good word for you before the job even becomes officially open. Better yet, your company contact might be able to convince everyone that there's no need to go through the expense of recruiting for a position when someone as well qualified as you is already available and interested. *That* would be something worth tweeting about.

Blogs

Though not a social networking site, blogs are still an effective way to build contacts and create an online presence that will impress employers. A blog goes well beyond the 140 characters or so that Twitter allows. The term comes from the phrase "web log" and refers to a website you create where you share your thoughts in pieces that generally run a few paragraphs. Before starting your own blog to emphasize some of your green efforts, you should become very familiar with established green bloggers.

Perhaps the best place to start when it comes to finding green bloggers is a website that compiles and rates the best green blog sites: www.bestgreenblogs.com. Here you'll find a wide range of bloggers listed as well as a clear description of what areas these bloggers focus on. You can subscribe to their feeds and receive alerts and links whenever new content is added. These bloggers will provide you with lots of advice on how to live greener and reduce your carbon footprint. They also will keep you informed on the latest green news. Following are just a few green blogs that might interest you:

- **The Ecopreneurist (http://ecopreneurist.com)** focuses on news and advice on sustainable and social entrepreneurship with news on green marketing, startups, and branding issues.

- **BusinessGreen (www.businessgreen.com)** offers blogs as well as information on controversial issues, green IT, and the green workplace.

- **The University of Illinois Sustainable Technology Center** offers a website called "News Bits" (http://lib.wmrc.uiuc.edu/enb/) that will point you to green content and some bloggers.

- **Linda Barnes' Blog lines (www.bloglines.com/public/lbarnes)** provides links and abstracts to green bloggers' content. You can subscribe to the service free and read green blogs you likely never would have found without some guidance.

- **The Bioenergy Blog (http://thebioenergyblog.blogspot.com)** maintained by Gerry McKieman at the University of Iowa keeps readers up to date on the latest news on bioethanol and biodiesel fuels.

Green companies also often have their own blogs. You can find a list of some green companies in the Ultimate Green List (www.ultimategreenlist. com). Over time you'll identify key bloggers who match your interests. You can communicate with them, respond to their comments, and begin to build relationships with them and with others who read your comments. Before you know it, you'll feel like you're part of the greater green community and find yourself growing more and more passionate about your field. That passion and commitment will be apparent when you interview for a green job.

Starting Your Own Blog

You can easily start your own blog at Wordpress.com. A blog is a chance for you to write about what you really care about. Soon people who share your interests will discover you, and they will begin adding their comments. Recruiters are likely also to look at your blog if you provide a link on your resume, Facebook page, Twitter profile, and so on. It all contributes to your online presence, which in turn makes you more marketable.

Blogs require a lot of work, however. You have to refresh the content regularly or people will find it boring and stop visiting the site. It represents a sizable time commitment, but the sense of community and the increased self-marketing can be worth it.

Hybrid Networking Is the Most Powerful Approach

Networking in person and social networking via the Internet are complementary approaches. Used together, they make a very powerful tool for improving your chances of finding a great job in a tight economy. Networking in person is effective because it requires fewer "touches" for people to believe they know you. Personal charisma is difficult to generate via the Internet.

The strength of Internet social networking is its sheer scope. It takes longer to build up a relationship, but the fact you can connect with someone in a city you've never even visited is a big advantage.

Hundreds, even thousands, of people are out there who are simply friends you haven't met yet. You only have to let them know who you are and what you are interested in, and they will help you achieve your goals.

CHAPTER 8

Writing Your Resume and Cover Letter

Whether you print it and mail it or send it electronically, your resume is often the first real picture of you that an employer sees. To be useful, it must make a good impression immediately because most reviewers decide within 20–30 seconds whether they are interested in interviewing you. This chapter will take you through the parts of your resume and cover letter, paying particular attention to how career changers can retool these documents to get the best results.

What Does a Resume Do?

A resume tells the prospective employer what you have accomplished in the past and what you can do for his company now. The purpose of a resume is to get you an interview by selling your experience to an employer and quickly demonstrating that your skills match the exact ones he is looking for. You are marketing yourself and the resume is your sales brochure!

When to Use a Resume

If you've followed our advice and taken advantage of all of the networking opportunities discussed in the previous chapters, then chances are the employer you want to work for is aware of you. Maybe you were referred by a friend or colleague. Maybe you met at a career fair or conference. Maybe you just responded to the company's blog. Either way, it helps to have made some kind of contact before your resume hits an employer's desk.

But just because an employer knows your name doesn't mean he or she is aware of your credentials. The resume is primarily your ticket to an interview, but it proves useful in many situations.

Responding to a Job Ad

The employer provides a list of wants and needs in the job ad. She is usually looking for the "ideal" person and so she asks for everything. Michele tells her job seekers that if they match 80% of what an employer asks for, go for the job! The employer will probably not find the ideal person, but with the job market being in the employer's favor, she can ask for a lot and not expect to pay extra for it. She will not only want you to have the skills she is looking for, but she will want someone who is a good "fit" for the corporate culture, someone who will smoothly transition into the team and quickly make a positive contribution.

The most effective resumes are tailored or *targeted* to a particular employer. A "targeted" resume means that each resume you send out is different and specific to that employer's needs. It uses keywords from the job description and matches them directly to your past experience and accomplishments. If the job requirements listed in the ad are vague or unclear, you can try contacting someone who works for that company who can tell you what the company typically looks for in a candidate.

Networking

A resume is also used as a networking tool. If you have a conversation with someone and she seems interested in you, you can ask her if she would like your resume as a follow-up. She might even ask you first!

Interviewing

Your resume also acts as a "script" for both you and the employer in the interview. When you compose your resume, keep in mind that *you* choose the topics that you want to discuss. So if you had a bad work experience at one employer, you could choose to leave it out. Be prepared to expand on the accomplishments you listed, and be sure to show the employer how these accomplishments are relevant to the company. He wants to know how hiring you can help him solve *the company's* problems.

Screening Tool

Most of all, employers use resumes to decide who to interview. Employers look at resumes and quickly eliminate those that don't match what they are looking for. The goal of your resume is to get you screened in, not out.

What to Include on Your Resume

You'll need to spend some time and effort if you want a resume that will work for you. There are two types of information that you will need before you get started.

> **Information about yourself:** You'll need a clear understanding of your job skills, work history, education, and career goals. The information you learned through the assessment in Chapter 3 will help you identify your skills, personal traits, and work values.

> **Information about the job:** Gather as much information as possible about the position and the company to which you are applying. Your resume should show that your skills, education, work experience, and past job achievements have qualified you for this exact position. Remember your transferable skills when changing careers to a new "green" job.

It also is important to remember that many companies now use screening software that filters applicants' resumes based on keywords related to a job description. It is critical to include as many terms as possible that appear in the original job description. If the job description specifically mentions knowledge of C++ programming, for example, be sure that your resume reflects that knowledge if you have it; never assume that a company official will take the time to infer something that is not stated.

> **Painter's Tip:** If you are writing a resume or applying for a job while still employed, be sure to use a personal e-mail address and not a company e-mail address because the courts have held that no privacy is guaranteed for your e-mail when it is on a company server.

Types of Resumes

All of the resume styles in books and computer programs are variations and combinations of two formats: *reverse chronological* and *functional* resumes. The key to writing an effective resume is choosing the right style for you, one that emphasizes your strengths and de-emphasizes your weaknesses. Whichever resume style you choose, make sure you include examples of skills and accomplishments that are specifically related to the position you are seeking. Employers want to see measurable achievements. They want to see how you will contribute to their bottom line.

The Reverse Chronological Resume

This format lists the jobs you've had by dates of employment, starting with your most recent job and going backwards (no more than 10–15 years).

This format stresses what you accomplished in each of the positions you held. Make sure you include your transferable skills. You can find a sample reverse chronological resume on page 132 (Figure 8.1).

Use a reverse chronological resume if:

- You have steadily progressed up a career ladder and are looking for career advancement.
- You have recent experience in the field you are seeking.
- You have a continuous work history in your field.

The following worksheet can help you collect and compose the information you need to complete a chronological resume. Fill it out; then compare what you have with the sample resume that follows.

CHRONOLOGICAL RESUME WORKSHEET

Name_____

Street Address _____

City, State, ZIP _____

Phone Number(s) _____

E-mail _____

OBJECTIVE

_____

_____

SUMMARY

_____

_____

_____

_____

(continued)

(continued)

WORK EXPERIENCE

Employer _____

City, State _____

Dates _____

Job Title _____

Responsibilities

_____

_____

_____

_____

Accomplishments

- List your proudest accomplishment

_____

- List another accomplishment

_____

- Another accomplishment

_____

Employer _____

City, State _____

Dates _____

Job Title _____

Responsibilities

_____

_____

_____

_____

Accomplishments

- List your proudest accomplishment

_____

- List another accomplishment

_____

- Another accomplishment

_____

EDUCATION

School _____

City, State _____

Degree/Certificate _____

Date completed _____

School _____

City, State _____

Degree/Certificate _____

Date completed _____

List professional certificates or licenses if they are needed for the position.

_____

_____

_____

Jason Ruiz
123 Anystreet Road
San Jose, CA 90281
Cell (132) 509-6000
jasonruiz341z@yahoo.com

Objective: Seeking a **Project Manager** position in a "green" company

Skills/ Qualifications

Project Planning	Bilingual (English/Spanish)
Regulatory Compliance	Data Analysis
Scope-of-Work Evaluations	Multi-Level Collaboration
Cost Estimation	Team Leadership
Budget Management	Board-Level Reporting

Professional Experience and Achievements

Green Environmental   San Jose, CA   2006–Present
(A $1.5M environmental restoration and water isolation company)

Senior Project Manager
Lead multi-million dollar projects supervising 10 team members in defining project requirements, developing plans, and establishing safety and quality assurance guidelines. Oversee extensive field testing and identify and use cutting-edge environmental technologies to fulfill company business objectives. Develop status reports for presentation to senior management and Board of Directors. Recognized for consistent on-time and on-budget project delivery.

Major Accomplishments:
- Led turnaround of $1.5M project by improving testing process; delivered project 2 weeks ahead of schedule.
- Saved $400K by leading effective negotiations with top vendors.
- Achieved or surpassed all project milestones by dramatically improving inter-departmental communication and collaborative processes.
- Won Employee of the Year Award in 2009 for outstanding performance.

All-Green Engineering   Santa Clara, CA   2002–2006
(A $3M provider of environmental services)

Project Manager
Ensured compliance to statewide environmental measures by overseeing all environmental safety, health, and quality regulations and integrating them into project plans. Led 10-person team in analyzing technical requirements, devising solutions and determining appropriate methodologies for execution. Achieved on-time/on-budget delivery for projects valued at up to $2M. Managed $750K departmental budget.

Figure 8.1: A "Green" Reverse Chronological Resume Sample

Major Accomplishments
- Generated $90K in new business by identifying opportunities with potential and existing customers.
- Chosen to lead large-scale, high-profile government projects; positioned project management group as industry leader.

Education

University of California   Davis, CA   2001
Bachelor of Science in Environmental Engineering

Professional Development

Project Management Professional (PMP) Project Management Institute   2002
OSHA Hazardous Training Program   2006

Professional Membership

Northern California Environmental Protection Society

Enhancing a Chronologically Organized Resume

Some people want to move into a green industry but still perform the same basic function as their previous job. That's the case with Suzanne Smith, whose resume follows (Figure 8.2 on page 135). Sales management requires the same basic skills and experience regardless of the type of products being sold. Clearly, though, knowledge of green technology makes it much easier to sell such products, so Ms. Smith emphasizes that knowledge in her resume.

The key to her resume is Suzanne's desire to demonstrate transferrable skills. She has tailored this resume for a particular company and job opening and is careful to emphasize her recent green training. Let's look at some specific points Suzanne makes in her resume:

- Her objective spells out the specific position that she is targeting.

- She emphasizes her regional sales management experience in her "Summary of Qualifications" because she is applying for a similar position.

- Her "Summary of Qualifications" also emphasizes her knowledge of solar energy technology, clearly an advantage for a company in that field.

- She emphasizes her most relevant experience—as a regional sales manager—by moving it up to the first bullet item so that it is sure to be noticed by someone screening resumes.

- In the "Education" section, Suzanne further emphasizes the relevance of her certificate in environmental studies by highlighting the fact that the program included study of solar energy technology.

Simply listing a company's name and your latest job title does not do you justice. You need to show that you've grown and progressed within the company by listing your accomplishments, promotions, and awards, as Suzanne does with every bullet.

Chronological Resumes Are Not Always a Career Changer's Best Friend

If, like Suzanne, you are looking to make a lateral move into a green career, a chronological resume should work for you. For most readers of this book, however, it's probably not the best approach.

There are several reasons why a chronologically organized resume is not ideal for career changers:

- The companies you worked for, even if they are well known in your old career, probably will not garner any added points from a company official in your new career field.

- The emphasis on a chronological listing of jobs in your former career could stereotype you in the eyes of your potential interviewer. You don't want to be seen as a *former* teacher or a *former* financial analyst or a *former* customer-relations specialist so much as someone who has specific skills that are desirable.

- Gaps on a chronological resume look particularly bad. It's no longer a stigma to have suffered periods of unemployment, but it's best to put such time periods in the best light. If you took classes or received training during the time you were unemployed, be sure to include that information.

Painter's Tip: It doesn't take a genius to notice a year's gap between two jobs on a chronological resume. However, simply extending the dates of one job to cover a period of unemployment is not acceptable because it is dishonest and will be discovered when your old companies are contacted.

Suzanne Smith
150 West Bloomberg Street, Apartment 4B
New York, New York 10021
Home Phone: (212) 554-4532 / Cell: (212) 245-2243
E-mail: Suzanne_Smith@yahoo.com

CAREER OBJECTIVE

Regional Sales Manager, Envirocom Corporation

SUMMARY OF QUALIFICATIONS

Experienced sales management professional with documented success developing new business and managing regional operations. Skilled at developing new territories, selling at the CEO level, and exceeding sales quotas. Certificate in environmental studies, including courses in solar energy technology.

PROFESSIONAL EXPERIENCE

Widget World, Inc.   Chicago, Illinois   2005–Present
Sales Manager, Senior Account Executive

- Manage regional office of 12 account executives.
- Spearheaded international expansion into Latin American region, now second only to North America in revenue.
- Spurred new business development including signing five top distributors; increased channel sales from 5% to 25%.
- Top sales producer the past three years.

Axon Corporation   Chicago, Illinois   1997–2005
Account Executive

- Revenue leader; voted salesperson of the year four times.
- Successfully led sales initiative to introduce new product line.
- Managed successful trade show campaign that led to signing of six new sales partners that opened up four new vertical markets and increased sales 20%.
- Developed innovative business-to-business sales campaign based on social networking.

EDUCATION

City College of New York
Certificate in Environmental Studies, including solar energy 2005

New York University
B.A. Business Administration 1997

Figure 8.2: Reverse Chronological Resume for a "Lateral" Move to a Green Industry

- If you have had several *different* jobs in your old career, the fact that you have been a "job hopper" becomes readily apparent. It also makes for a very odd looking resume.

If any of the preceding describes you, then a functional resume may be the way to go.

The Functional (Skills-Based) Resume

This format emphasizes your skills and accomplishments as they relate to the job you are pursuing. A functional resume presents a profile of your experience based on professional strengths or skill groupings. Your employment history follows, but in less detail than in a chronological resume.

You should use this format if

- You have worked for only one employer but have held several job titles.

- You are applying for a type of job that is different from your present or previous job.

- You have little or no job experience (recent graduate). If this applies, emphasize your leadership or organizational skills in school (clubs, fraternity).

- You have gaps in your work history.

- You are re-entering the job market after a long break.

Do not use this format if:

- Your work history is stable and continuous, because employers sometimes assume that a functional resume hides a spotty, unstable work history.

Following is a worksheet you can use to begin creating your own functional resume, as well as sample functional "green" resumes you can use as models (Figures 8.3 and 8.4).

FUNCTIONAL RESUME WORKSHEET

Name_____

Street Address _____

City, State, ZIP _____

Phone Number(s) _____

E-mail _____

OBJECTIVE

_____

_____

SUMMARY

_____

_____

SKILLS

Skill _____

(Strongest skill needed for the position you are seeking)

List three accomplishments using this skill.

- _____

- _____

- _____

Skill _____

(Another skill needed for the position you are seeking)

List three accomplishments using this skill.

- _____

- _____

- _____

(continued)

(continued)

Skill_____

(Another skill needed for the position you are seeking)

List three accomplishments using this skill.

- _____

- _____

- _____

EMPLOYMENT HISTORY

Company_____

City, State _____

Dates Worked _____

Title_____

_____

Company_____

City, State _____

Dates Worked _____

Title_____

EDUCATION

School _____ City, State_____

Degree/Certificate _____

List professional certificates or licenses if they are needed for the position.

_____

_____

Jason Ruiz
123 Anystreet Road
San Jose, CA 90281
Cell (132) 509-6000
jasonruiz341z@yahoo.com

Objective: Seeking a **Project Manager** position in a "green" company

Skills/Qualifications

Project Leadership

- Lead multi-million dollar projects.
- Supervise 10 team members.
- Achieved or surpassed all project milestones by dramatically improving inter-departmental communication and collaborative processes.
- Hand-picked to lead large-scale, high-profile government projects.
- Won "Employee of the Year" award.

Regulatory Compliance

- Complied with state environmental initiatives.
- Oversaw all environmental safety, health, and quality regulations and ensured they were integrated into project plans.

Project Planning

- Define project requirements, develop plans for execution, and establish safety and quality assurance guidelines.
- Identify and oversee extensive field testing and cutting-edge environmental technologies to achieve project objectives.
- Led turnaround of $1M project by improving the testing process.
- Saved $400K by leading effective negotiation with top vendors.

Budget Management

- Achieved on-time/on-budget delivery of projects
- Managed $750K departmental budget
- Generated $90K in new business

Professional Experience

Green Environmental   San Jose, CA   2006–Present
(A $1.5M environmental restoration and water isolation company)
Senior Project Manager

(continued)

Figure 8.3: A "Green" Functional Resume

(continued)

All-Green Engineering   Santa Clara, CA   2002–2006
(A $3M provider of environmental services)
Project Manager

Education

University of California   Davis, CA   2001
Bachelor of Science in Environmental Engineering

Professional Development

Project Management Professional (PMP) Project Management Institute   2002
OSHA Hazardous Training Program   2006

Professional Membership

Northern California Environmental Protection Society

You can compare Jason's chronological resume (page 132) with his functional one to see the difference in approach.

Now let's look at another example, that of John Ridgemont, who has had a few jobs but no real career. He has credentialed himself in the area of green technology and is seeking a technical writing position in a green industry. Figure 8.4 shows John's resume.

There are a number of things to notice about this resume. First, the career goal has been made very specific: a specific job title with a specific company. Second, John has spotlighted his accomplishments and skills due to his spotty work history. These represent the transferable skills that make John qualified for his new career position despite his lack of previous experience in the field.

Notice that the "Accomplishments and Skills" section addresses the key question an interviewer is bound to have: Why should I even consider a person with such a different background? The answer is that the content in this section matches up precisely with the major skills required in the company's job description.

Note that while John has not actually done any technical writing, his resume argues that he has done professional-level writing *and* he has knowledge of the technical writing software he is likely to use. Furthermore, he has a knowledge of the latest green technology that he would be expected to write about.

John Ridgemont
1010 West Huckleberry Lane
Phoenix, Arizona 85021
Home Phone: (876) 444-4532 / Cell: (876) 542-2243
E-mail: john_ridgemont@me.com

Career Objective: Technical Editor for Eco-Assure

Accomplishments and Skills

Writing Skills
- Wrote the City of Vista annual report on race relations.
- Wrote customer handbook for new salespeople, nationally distributed.
- Wrote widely disseminated City of Vista report analyzing support for the homeless.

Technical Writing Software Expertise
- Knowledge of FrameMaker
- Knowledge of Microsoft Word, Excel, PowerPoint, and Access
- Knowledge of PC and Macintosh hardware

Knowledge of Green Technology
- Completed rigorous 12-month certificate program covering major green technology.

Professional Experience

City of Vista **Administrative Analyst**	Vista, CA	2009–2011
Xytel Corporation **Customer Relations Specialist**	Los Angeles, CA	2005–2009
Radio Shack **Salesman**	Los Angeles, CA	2001–2005

Other Related Experience

- Explained complex electronics to customers; boosted in-store sales by 10%.
- Wrote and published monthly local Rainforest Alliance newsletter with 1,500-member circulation.
- Interviewed 100 respondents for senior project at Arizona State University.
- Led team at Xytel; received highest customer satisfaction evaluation.

Education

Arizona State University **B.S. Political Science with Distinction**	Tempe, Arizona	2000

Figure 8.4: A Functional Resume for a Career Changer

The Combination Resume

We said earlier that there were essentially two kinds of resumes, but you can combine them as well. A combination resume lists your skills and experience first, followed by a chronological work history. With this type of resume you can highlight the skills you have that are relevant to the job you are applying for *and* provide the work history that employers prefer. Figure 8.5 illustrates the changes you would make to John Ridgemont's resume to turn it into a combination resume. Whereas in a functional resume employment history is very brief—a simple line-by-line listing—a combination resume includes bulleted highlights of accomplishments in each position.

For many career changers a combination resume is the best of both worlds. It provides an opportunity to address the question of why a company should consider you in its opening section by pointing out the skills you bring. Plus the employment section is fuller, which provides ample opportunity to highlight major accomplishments.

DON'T BE GENERIC

We mentioned earlier that you should write a customized resume for each company and position. With today's computer software it is easy to create a generic resume that you then modify based on a company's specific job description. This allows you to include the keywords the employer uses in the want ad and to respond directly to that company's needs. Granted, targeted resumes take a little longer than clicking and sending a generic resume, but it will pay off in more interviews if you do it right!

Writing Your Resume, Section by Section

Now that you have some idea of the types of resumes you could create and most of the information you need to write one, it's time to take it step by step, looking closely at each part of the resume and how you can adapt it to meet your needs.

Painter's Tip: Listing a cell phone number allows the employer/recruiter to contact you anytime. When listing an e-mail, make sure it sounds professional or generic, not "cute." And while you are at it, check your voice mail recording to be sure it sounds professional, too.

John Ridgemont
1010 West Huckleberry Lane
Phoenix, Arizona 85021
Home Phone: (876) 444-4532 / Cell: (876) 542-2243
E-mail: john_ridgemont@me.com

Career Objective: Technical Editor for Eco-Assure

Accomplishments and Skills

Writing and Editing Skills
- Researched, wrote, and published four 200-page reports for city agency.
- Wrote and edited monthly newsletter distributed to more than 1,500 subscribers.
- Interviewed 100 respondents, analyzed results, and wrote 150-page report on impact of marketing environmental products to college students.

Technical Writing Software Expertise
- Knowledge of FrameMaker
- Knowledge of Microsoft Word, Excel, PowerPoint, and Access
- Knowledge of PC and Macintosh hardware

Knowledge of Green Technology
- Completed rigorous 12-month certificate program covering major green technology.

Professional Experience

City of Vista   Vista, CA   2009–2011
Administrative Analyst
- Wrote widely disseminated City of Vista report analyzing support for the homeless.
- Wrote the City of Vista annual report on race relations.

Xytel Corporation   Los Angeles, CA   2005–2009
Customer Relations Specialist
- Led team at Xytel; received highest customer satisfaction evaluation.
- Worked independently to solve customer issues; received highest evaluation.

Radio Shack   Los Angeles, CA   2001–2005
Salesman
- Wrote customer handbook for new salespeople, nationally distributed.
- Explained complex electronics to customers; boosted in-store sales by 10%.

Education

Arizona State University   Tempe, Arizona   2000
B.S. Political Science with Distinction

Figure 8.5: A Combination Resume for a Career Changer

Special Skills

Special skills (such as typing 90 words a minute; speaking Spanish, French, or Japanese; and so on) should always be presented upfront so a hiring manager knows what you can do (provided they are relevant to the job, of course). You can create a section to showcase these skills. Following are some skills you might include:

- Computer proficiencies

- Office procedures (answering multi-line phones, transcription, 10-key, and so on)

- Language abilities (fluency in a foreign language, translation ability)

- Any skill that is industry specific for the job you are seeking (such as regulatory compliance, environmental safety and health oversight, project management, and so on)

Job Objective

A job objective tells the reader what type of position you are seeking. If you have a specific job in mind and can tailor your resume accordingly, state a job objective at the beginning of the resume. In order for a job objective to be meaningful, it should be as specific as possible.

You'll want to avoid a job objective statement that sounds like this:

"Seeking a challenging position in a high-growth green organization that will allow me to use my transferable skills and experience"

Or this:

"A position in engineering that will maximize my talents"

These job objectives are too vague. If the recruiter can't figure out immediately what you are applying for, he will discard your resume, reading no further.

Here are some well-written, more *specific* job objectives:

"An operations position in a solar panel manufacturing company"

"A senior management position in bio-diesel manufacturing"

Summary Statement

Your summary statement (which is optional) describes your qualifications and experience in a short paragraph that appears at the beginning of the resume. It "sums up" who you are. Because the average length of time an employer spends scanning a resume is 20–30 seconds, orienting the reader quickly to who you are and what you have to offer is essential. This can be used in place of the skills or qualification section.

The summary statement should be brief (maybe three sentences) but should include your skill strengths, areas of expertise, and functional specialties; and the length and breadth of your experience.

Here are two examples of well-written "green" summary statements:

LEED Certified Air-Sealing Technician specializing in residential home construction. Nine years of homebuilding/insulation experience reinforced by an AA degree in Engineering, LEED Green Associate certification, LEED Accredited Professional credential, and a passion for energy conservation.

Project Management Professional with 9+ years of experience in managing multi-million dollar environmental projects, building high-performing cross-functional teams, and optimizing project resources to achieve significant cost savings. Adept at assessing customer needs to determine project scope, budget, and schedule; dedicated to ensuring regulatory compliance and achieving quality deliverables. Proven problem solver using cutting-edge technologies to positively impact company bottom line.

Professional Experience

In this section you list your previous employers, their city and state, the dates worked, and the job title you held in reverse chronological order. Keep the following in mind as you record your work history:

- Hiring managers prefer years of employment, rather than months (2007–2010 rather than March 2007–April 2010). Dates should go on the right side of the page.

- You should include daily duties and responsibilities, as well as greatest accomplishments. A bullet format is preferred. Delete unnecessary articles and adjectives. Phrases should be short and snappy. Begin each phrase with an action verb (initiated, supervised, developed, and so on), such as "lowered energy costs, increased comfort levels, and improved indoor air quality using proper air-sealing techniques."

- For jobs where you are still employed, write your job duties in the present tense. For jobs held in the past, write your responsibilities in the past tense.

- If you have more than 15 years of experience, you need not list every job. It is likely that an interviewer would view your earlier jobs as irrelevant because conditions change so quickly in the business world. Another reason for not listing all your earlier jobs is that you don't want to come across as too old, particularly for a new career.

- You don't want to be stereotyped by your job titles, especially in another career field. Put the emphasis not on the job titles but on the functions you performed, particularly those that are transferable to your new career field.

Education and Training

In this section you list schools and training attended, city and state, degrees and certifications, and dates for schooling that pertain to the job you're seeking.

If you are an entry-level candidate with little or no professional experience, your education should be presented immediately after your skills or qualification summary. This is because your education is your most marketable asset. Here you can include:

- Your GPA (if 3.5 or higher)

- Awards/scholarships you won

- If you made the Dean's list

- Coursework relevant to the job

If you are a professional with more than five years of experience, education should be listed last on your resume. GPAs, awards, scholarships, and such are not usually mentioned in this case.

RESUME DOS AND DON'TS

Do:

- Be positive and "sell" yourself.

- Identify your relative accomplishments and quantify them where applicable; describe how they benefit the employer.

- Have friends who know you professionally read your resume and suggest any accomplishments that were forgotten.

- Be specific, choose your words carefully, and eliminate unnecessary words.

- Use concise bullet phrases that are easy to read.

- Use action words.

- Put the most important data at the top left of the resume.

- Proofread carefully and have someone else proofread it. Make sure spelling, grammar, and punctuation are flawless.

- Type your resume and print it "letter quality" on white or cream-colored paper. Paper 24 lb. weight with cotton content is preferred.

- Use wide margins. Single space sections, double space between sections.

- Use Times New Roman or Ariel 11- or 12-point font.

- Center or justify lines and capitalize or bold all headings.

- Make sure your resume "looks good" (neat, readable, symmetrical, and visually balanced.

Don't:

- List items not directly related to the position you seek (personal data, hobbies).

- Use more than a few lines to describe your accomplishments.

- Try to explain employment gaps or reasons for leaving a job.

- Include references. Instead put three to five references on a separate page and give it to the employer when requested.

- Bury the most important information at the bottom of the resume—bring it to the top.

- Include salary requirements.

- Use abbreviations except for names of states.

Accomplishments

Nothing on your resume is more important than your accomplishments. In a "buyer's market," such as we have now, the hiring manager has *hundreds* of candidates clamoring for the position. If each candidate has the same basic education and professional background, who gets the job? Usually it's the candidate who contributed the most at past positions! Your accomplishments are what separate you from other equally qualified candidates.

Not everything you do at work should be considered an accomplishment, though. For example, just making it to work everyday isn't an accomplishment (though sometimes it sure feels like it). Resume-worthy accomplishments include

- Increasing the company's bottom line
- Streamlining procedures
- Earning promotions
- Special projects completed successfully
- Decreasing costs
- Company- or industry-sponsored awards
- Certifications and licensures

What is *not* an accomplishment?

- Daily responsibilities (your job description)
- Regular attendance
- Volunteer/community service unless it has a direct bearing on your job search
- Getting along with coworkers
- Working full-time while going to school at night

In short, an accomplishment is something that "goes beyond" your usual job description.

For it to have the greatest impact, an accomplishment should be quantified. A quantified accomplishment is one that includes dollar figures, percentages, numbers, and time periods. For example: "Streamlined procedures resulting in $2,000 monthly savings within three months of hire." The dollar figure quantifies the accomplishment while the "streamlined procedures" explains how he did it. Because he achieved those savings within three months of hire, that further strengthens his accomplishment.

You can use the following questions to help you remember some of your accomplishments. Also, you can go back to Chapter 3 and review the accomplishments you used to identify your best skills.

- Did you identify a problem and solve it? What were the results?

- Did you introduce a new procedure that made work easier or more accurate?

- Did your efforts increase the company's profits? By how much?

- Did you increase productivity or reduce downtime? By how much?

- Did you effectively manage systems or people? What were the results?

- Did you initiate a sales or incentive program that worked? What were the results in dollars and cents? In company image? In terms of morale?

- Did you participate in major decision making or planning? What contribution did you make to the team? What were the results of your efforts?

- Did you improve the efficiency of people or operations? What were the savings?

- Did you automate any systems or procedures? How much money was involved in the automation?

As you go to list your accomplishments on your resume, feel free to scour the list of action verbs that follows for inspiration.

AN ACTION-PACKED RESUME (VERBS, THAT IS)

The following are action verbs you might find helpful in describing your accomplishments and skills in your resume.

accomplished	commended	delivered	evaluated
achieved	communicated	demonstrated	examined
acquired	compared	designed	executed
activated	compiled	detected	expanded
adapted	composed	determined	expedited
addressed	computed	developed	explained
adjusted	conceived	devised	expressed
administered	conceptualized	diagnosed	extracted
advanced	condensed	directed	fabricated
advised	conducted	discovered	facilitated
allocated	conserved	dispensed	fashioned
analyzed	consolidated	displayed	filed
approved	constructed	distributed	financed
arranged	consulted	diverted	fixed
assembled	contacted	documented	followed up
assessed	contracted	drafted	forecasted
assigned	contributed	earned	formed
assisted	controlled	edited	formulated
assured	converted	eliminated	found
attained	cooperated	employed	functioned as
attended	coordinated	enacted	gained
augmented	correlated	encouraged	gathered
balanced	corroborated	enforced	generated
brought about	counseled	engineered	governed
built	created	enhanced	guided
calculated	cultivated	enlisted	handled
clarified	dealt	ensured	headed
coached	decided	equipped	hired
collected	defined	establish	identified
commanded	delegated	estimated	illustrated

improved	monitored	promoted	scheduled
increased	motivated	proposed	screened
influenced	negotiated	protected	secured
informed	observed	proved	selected
initiated	obtained	provided	separated
inspected	offered	publicized	served
inspired	operated	purchased	serviced
installed	optimized	questioned	set up
instigated	orchestrated	realized	shaped
instilled	ordered	received	shifted
instituted	organized	recognized	shipped
instructed	originated	recommended	simplified
insured	overcame	reconciled	sold
integrated	oversaw	recorded	solidified
interfaced	participated	recruited	solved
interpreted	perceived	referred	sorted
interviewed	perfected	refined	spoke
introduced	performed	regulated	stimulated
invented	persuaded	rehabilitated	stored
investigated	piloted	related	streamlined
judged	pioneered	rendered	structured
justified	placed	reorganized	substituted
kept	planned	repaired	succeeded
launched	played	reported	summarized
lectured	predicted	represented	supervised
led	prepared	researched	supplied
lifted	prescribed	resolved	synthesized
located	presented	responded	tested
logged	prevented	restored	trained
maintained	printed	retrieved	transformed
managed	processed	reviewed	unified
mastered	produced	revised	
mediated	programmed	revitalized	
minimized	projected	saved	

Electronic Resumes

Often you will be asked to attach a copy of your resume as part of an on-line application or as part of an e-mail request. The problem is that much of the formatting you labored over for your print resume could be lost when an interviewer opens the attachment depending on the software used.

For this reason, you will need to create a version of your resume suitable for electronic submission—one that is free of all the fancy formatting. Keep the following in mind as you create an electronic version of your resume:

- Don't use boldface, italics, or underlines.
- Don't include any graphics.
- Don't use tabs. Use the spacebar to center text.
- Use 12-point Arial font.
- Don't press the Return key at the end of a line.
- Create the resume in your word processing program and then save the document as plain text. Select the option to insert line breaks. You will be warned that you could lose some formatting. Click "OK."
- Use a text editor such as Notepad on the PC or SimpleText on the Macintosh and open your reformatted resume. You may need to clean it up a bit.
- Move items flush with the left margin.
- Make sure your contact information is on separate lines.
- Consider using all capitals where you previously used boldface.
- Ensure that you have replaced bullets with asterisks.

Employer Resume-Creating Applications

Unfortunately, some companies employ their own resume creating applications that force you to follow *their* chronological resume format. These websites often require you to register to apply and also require that you answer a series of questions about your work history. That's not always good for a career changer. If you are faced with such an application process, keep in mind the following:

- Often these websites still give you the option of uploading your own resume; if you have that option, take it.

- If you can only use the company's chronologically oriented resume format, take advantage of the fact that these sites often provide room for you to write a cover letter. Your cover letter will be your chance to emphasize your transferable skills. We will discuss cover letters shortly.

- Study the key terms found in the job description. Many of these websites use software that screens applications by awarding points if certain keywords are included. Try to include as many of the key terms found in the job description as possible in your resume and cover letter.

- Don't fill in the salary part of the employment history unless they force you to. This is something you negotiate *after* you are offered the job.

Tips for Using Your Resume

Following are a few final tips for getting your resume read:

- Resumes should be sent to a person by name. Avoid sending a resume to a job title such as "Production Manager." It will take extra effort, but do your research and find out the name and title of the appropriate person to send to.

- If you are asked to send your resume to human resources, do so. But also send a resume to the person in charge of the department in which you want to work. As we've said before, even if Human Resources does the screening, the department manager is the final hiring authority.

- When mailing, faxing, or e-mailing your resume, always send it with a cover letter. Never send it by itself.

- Mass mailing your resume to many employers hoping that it will get someone's attention is not effective. For every 1,000 resumes you send out, you can expect two interviews. An accepted standard is that for every ten interviews you will get one job offer. Do you have 5,000 employers you want to send your resume to?

- Look for ways to target your resume to the specific needs of the employer. This can be accomplished by a targeted resume or a cover letter.

- When researching employers, find out whether they use a resume scanning system. Knowing this can help you prepare your resume for presentation.

- Send your resume to employers even if they aren't hiring. You never know what the future will bring.

- Always follow up on your resume with a phone call. Be courteous and professional and sell your qualifications. Be sure to ask for an interview.

- When directly contacting employers, always have a copy of your resume available and offer it to them.

- When applying for a job with an application, you may want to attach a resume. Still, if you are asked to fill out an application, never write "see resume." Take the time to fill it out completely.

- Give a copy of your resume to your references. It provides them with current information about you.

By this point, you should be able to put together an outstanding "green" resume that will get you noticed and convince the employer to bring you in for an interview. But first, a quick word about putting in a *good* word.

Lining Up References

Before you begin your job search, it's important to line up several potential references. Depending on which specific skills or experiences you want to validate, certain colleagues will work better than others. Similarly, don't select a supervisor if you believe he or she cannot present you positively. Remember the following:

- Ask ahead of time how a particular reference wants to be contacted. Some don't mind being contacted at work while others will want to be contacted at home.

- Cast a broad net when it comes to references. You might want to substitute a colleague or even a manager other than your immediate supervisor if you feel that person will be more positive about your work. If a colleague has left the company, give yourself plenty of time to use social networking sources such as LinkedIn to locate the person and secure permission to use him or her as a reference.

- Look for potential references who are outgoing and enthusiastic. If you are currently employed and don't want to use your supervisor as a reference, look for ex-employees who can comment on your performance.

- If your past employer has a policy of not providing references and only verifying dates of employment, think about ex-colleagues and others who could comment on your employment record.

- Give all of your references a copy of your resume so that they will know how you are presenting yourself.

- Ask ahead of time whether your references feel comfortable emphasizing specific things you want them to talk about.

- When the time comes to provide references to a potential employer, make sure you call each reference first and reiterate what was discussed during the interview and what points you would like him or her to focus on.

- Be sure to follow up and thank your references after the company has contacted them. Give them the opportunity to provide you with feedback as to their conversations with your potential employer. Did the employer seem concerned about anything? Did he or she say anything to indicate you might get the job?

- Finally, let your references know if you get the job and send them a thank-you note regardless.

Writing Cover Letters

Submitting a resume without a cover letter is a waste of time. Think of it this way: You only have one shot at getting the attention of a company official who is screening applicants. Why not increase your chances by taking that person by the hand and leading him or her to specific parts of your resume and highlighting the relevance of these items to the job? That's essentially what a cover letter does.

You can use a cover letter to point to specific reasons that you should be considered. Let's say that you know someone in the company who has encouraged you to apply. Why not mention that person? Let's say that you are aware of a new direction the company is heading and you have just completed some courses that provide you with the latest knowledge of that technology. Why not call attention to that fact?

Cover letters are especially important for career changers. They *need* a cover letter to highlight why the company should bother looking at their resumes, particularly since they are likely very different from those of other applicants.

Your cover letter can bridge the gap between your past experience and your future career. More specifically, it can

- Call attention to specific courses you have completed recently that make you an ideal candidate.

- Call attention to tasks that you might have performed in your other career that exhibit transferable skills that are readily adaptable to your new one.

- Expand on any training you might have had in your previous career that is directly applicable to the job. Examples could include training in management and supervision, communications skills, computer skills, and so on.

Even more than resumes, cover letters need to be individualized for each company to which you are applying. Still, the format generally is the same:

1. A first paragraph introducing yourself and indicating the specific position to which you are applying.

2. A middle paragraph that highlights your relevant background and experience and indicates why you are worth pursuing. This is the paragraph where you can point to how the company's direction matches up with your capabilities. You can also refer to your resume and call attention to points worth emphasizing or clarifying.

3. A final paragraph that asks for an interview, clarifies when you are available and how to contact you, and expresses your enthusiasm and appreciation.

To see how to craft a cover letter, let's first take a look at the job description in Figure 8.6.

XCC is looking for a **Program Administrator** to work in our Los Angeles office to serve in a key role facilitating the flow of information between the Program Managers, XCC corporate headquarters, the program sponsors, the public, and outside energy efficiency groups and organizations.

The **Program Administrator** will be responsible for:

- Authorizing work proposals as well as payments to contractors for job completions under the Home Performance program. This includes reviewing the contractor's inputs into the program's software to ensure that it is complete, correct, and adequately records critical pre- and post-installation measurements and health and safety tests; verifying homeowner's incentive status; maintaining electric and physical files holding records of all program jobs; assisting contractors in resolving any problems related to job scope and/or data input; referring issues to XCC management for further action as appropriate.
- Processing program incentive claims.
- Preparing or assisting in the preparation of program reports and briefings, both internally and to LIPA.
- Creating, editing, and updating program materials and information pieces.
- Handling customer inquiries and complaints efficiently and professionally.
- Contributing to program recruiting efforts by speaking with contractors on the phone, conducting meetings, and delivering presentations, as appropriate. Updating and maintaining contractor contact records in program's contractor database.
- Providing program administrative and computer data entry support to contractors who have joined the program but need assistance or information on program design, rules, and procedure.

Requirements/Qualifications:

- 3–5 years demonstrated experience in administration.
- Excellent communication and interpersonal skills.
- Strong organizational skills.
- Candidate must demonstrate an ability to initiate, coordinate, and prioritize responsibilities and follow through on tasks and projects.
- Experience with Microsoft Office Suite is required and a familiarity with database entry and/or SQL language is desired.
- Experience with administering energy efficiency programs, and knowledge of energy-efficient technologies, health and safety, and residential contracting, are highly desired.
- Ability to perform multiple tasks in an environment of frequent and often short deadlines is required.

Position is fast paced and provides a high-energy opportunity for career growth and new learning opportunities. Salary Range: Commensurate with experience. Compensation package includes paid holidays, 80% paid medical, 50% paid dental, paid life & AD&D and paid STD & LTD insurance coverage, plus employer matching retirement plan.

Please apply online at: www.xcc.com/jobs.

XCC is an Equal Opportunity Employer.

Figure 8.6: An Advertised "Green" Job

Analyzing the Job Description

Before you can customize your resume for a position or draft a customized cover letter, you must first analyze the job description. In this case, the position is for a program coordinator for a company in a green industry. Let's assume you are a commercial loan representative. Analyzing this description, several items probably jump out at you:

- The position requires administrative experience. You realize you have these transferable skills even though you have not worked in this green industry.

- The position requires computer skills. You have this training from your previous career.

- The position requires numerous communications skills, including talking with customers and sponsors, writing and editing materials, and making presentations. Once again, all these skills can be transferred from your previous career.

- You have *not* worked with contractors in the building profession, but you *have* taken classes in green building construction and technology as part of the credential program you recently completed. Your training includes information on the latest green building standards.

- The position apparently requires a self-starter who can work independently and efficiently despite the need to deal with a lot of very detailed paperwork that needs to be processed.

- The position requires you to apply online. That means you probably have to use the company's resume builder software that would not give you a chance to emphasize your transferable skills. It is absolutely critical that you do so in a cover letter.

- Your resume and cover letter will likely have to be in plain text because they will have to be uploaded to the company's website. That means that both resume and cover letter will have to avoid the use of bullets, boldface, and graphics.

Crafting Your Cover Letter

Figure 8.7 shows a cover letter written in response to the Program Administer position. The cover letter is essential in order to show how the applicant qualifies for the job.

1005 West Valley Avenue
Los Angeles, California 90034
June 1, 20xx

Dear XCC Recruiter:

Please consider me for a **Program Administrator** position with XCC. My background includes extensive administrative and project management experience. In addition, I have recently completed an intensive credential program that included coursework in green building construction and technology. I am familiar with the latest green building construction standards. Finally, I have received the highest possible evaluation for my customer-relations skills.

At Widget Corporation I was responsible for creating, editing, and processing commercial loan documents involving multi-million dollar projects. In that position, I worked closely with a variety of different clients including banks, brokers, and customers. I frequently made presentations to potential customers and edited a company newsletter using Microsoft Office applications. When I worked for Higher Echelon Enterprises, I received training in SQL programming and was responsible for maintaining a company customer database.

My resume provides more details on my work experience. Recently I received a certificate in Environmental Science from California State University in Los Angeles. My coursework included training in LEED standards. Recently I earned the LEED Green Associate credential. I am excited about the possibility of being able to apply my training in the latest green building techniques and analyses and working closely with contractors for XCC.

I will contact you next week about setting up a time to discuss more thoroughly how my qualifications might benefit XCC.

Regards,

(Your name and contact information here)

Figure 8.7: Cover Letter Responding to the Job Advertisement

Note how the cover letter identifies the position; lists the skills and recent "green technology" coursework that relate to the job; and addresses the administrative, communication, and computer skills that the company is looking for. Even coming from another industry, the letter clearly points out why this person is the best candidate for the job.

Using a Cover Letter to Find Jobs

Every time you apply for an advertised job opening, hundreds, even thousands of other people do likewise. Unless you are extraordinarily qualified, it is very difficult to gain the attention of the screener and make it on the list of those applicants who will be interviewed. The key—as we've said all along—is to gain an advantage and apply for jobs that aren't advertised. A targeted cover letter can help you do just that.

Let's say that you have networked and found the name of a key contact with XCC Corporation, someone in the very department where program administrators work—except now let's assume there are no open positions posted on the company website. You have learned from another contact about a specific new set of projects on the horizon for the company, however. You have all the information you need to write a customized resume and cover letter.

But why bother if there are no positions currently being advertised? More often than you might think, companies will receive budget authorization to hire on very short notice. If a manager has a set of resumes he or she has collected, the company often will save the time and expense of advertising the position and will stick with people he already knows—people who have already sent him a brilliant resume and cover letter explaining why they are an ideal candidate—should such an opportunity arise.

Figure 8.8 shows much the same cover letter as you read previously, except this time it is fishing for an opportunity rather than responding to one.

Note that this cover letter begins by calling attention to the fact that you have been referred by someone already working in the department. The reference to an employee referral should encourage Mr. Bailey to read the rest of the letter. In addition, the cover letter points to knowledge of an upcoming major project for the company. The real key here is that there is a real person with the power to hire who has been identified and written to directly.

Note: It is absolutely critical to write to the person who has referred you, thank her, and let her know you have just sent a note to the person targeted. This way the referral can casually check with the boss and put in another good word.

There are four possible outcomes from such a letter. Let's take them one by one:

- Bailey replies that there is no current opening, but he will keep the letter and resume on file because something might open up in the immediate future. If you receive this note, write back in a month or so if you are still pursuing your job search.

- Bailey replies that he appreciates the letter, but there are no openings. You haven't really lost much except the price of a stamp and few minutes' time composing the letter.

- Bailey replies that the company is opening up a new job requisition and he'd like to arrange an interview. You hit the jackpot.

- Bailey never replies. Nothing ventured, nothing gained. Go ahead and wait a couple of weeks and then call Fred Bailey directly. There's always the chance the letter was buried or Bailey got caught up in some kind of crisis and never got around to responding. If it turns out Bailey simply had no intention of responding, that's good to know as well. Would you really want to work for someone who doesn't bother to respond even when there is a referral from someone in his or her own department?

Fred Bailey, New Construction Manager
XCC Corporation
1005 West Valley Avenue
Los Angeles, California 90034
June 1, 20xx

Dear Mr. Bailey,

Larry Rascal in your department suggested I send you a copy of my resume. I'm very excited about the upcoming LEED building construction project Larry described to me. I would appreciate it if you would consider me for a Program Administrator position should one open up. My background includes extensive administrative and project management experience. Larry indicated that you might be interested in my recent training in LEED building certification. I recently completed an intensive credential program at California State University in Los Angeles that included coursework in green building construction and technology. My coursework included training in LEED standards. Recently I earned the LEED Green Associate credential. Finally, I have received the highest possible evaluation for my customer-relations skills.

At Widget Corporation I was responsible for creating, editing, and processing commercial loan documents involving multi-million dollar projects. In that position, I worked closely with a variety of different clients including banks, brokers, and customers. I frequently made presentations to potential customers, and I also edited a company newsletter using Microsoft Office applications. When I worked for Higher Echelon Enterprises, I received training in SQL programming and was responsible for maintaining a company customer database.

I am excited about the possibility of being able to apply my training in the latest green building techniques and LEED energy analysis and help XCC succeed with its new LEED program.

I will contact you next week about setting up a time to discuss more thoroughly how my qualifications might benefit XCC.

Regards,

(Your name and contact information here)

Figure 8.8: Cover Letter for an Unadvertised Position

Cover letters, whether for an advertised or unadvertised position, are *your* ad for why you are the perfect candidate. They highlight the exact strengths and skills that the employer wants without having to hunt for them in the resume. A carefully crafted cover letter will greatly increase your chances of being selected for an interview—the next, and final stage in your quest for a green career.

CHAPTER 9

Overcoming Interview Challenges

You've made the right contacts, sent off your perfect resume, and landed the interview. Congratulations are in order. Now that you have the interview, what do you *do* with it? This chapter looks at ways you can optimize your interview and turn it into a job offer. It will lead you step-by-step through the process from the time you are asked for an interview until you negotiate your salary.

Along the way, we'll pay special attention to the unique issues career changers face during an interview, including how to handle the objections an interviewer might raise about your decision to change careers. In fact, interviews can be twice as nerve-wracking for career changers because they probably have never interviewed for a job in their new industry. This chapter will help you feel prepared and confident.

Two Ways to Ensure Success

As you will learn shortly, there are many different types of interviews. Regardless of how the interview is structured, here are a couple of important points to keep in mind:

- One of the two major reasons HR professionals reject an applicant is lack of enthusiasm. Even if you are not a "rah rah" type of person, it's critical that you bring a high level of enthusiasm to every aspect of the job search process. That means responding to even the request for an interview with excitement. It also means expressing your enthusiasm when you first meet the interviewer as well as at the conclusion of the interview and in your thank-you letter.

- The second major reason HR professionals say they reject applicants is for poor communication skills. Regardless of the industry or the position, applicants are expected to answer questions coherently and think on their feet. Perhaps the major reason applicants fail at this is because of poor listening skills. You need to practice active listening skills when being interviewed. Instead of thinking of your answer while the interviewer is talking, concentrate on understanding the question. If you are unsure, ask qualifying questions. It's fine to use a pad and pen to jot down the key aspects of the question or to write down a point or two you want to make. Of course it is also important to maintain eye contact when responding.

Keep these two strategies in mind—enthusiasm and good communication skills—as we walk through each step of the interview process.

Handling Interview Requests

Of course you're thrilled. After all the networking and searching, you've just received a call or e-mail requesting an interview. Remember that everything from this point on counts when it comes to making a good impression and securing a job offer. That means how you handle yourself over the phone and via e-mail is crucial. Keep the following in mind:

- Be professional over the phone. It's good to be excited, but also be polite. Be sure to have paper and a pen available near your phone so you can take notes carefully. In your excited state, you're prone to forget key details such as time, location, and so on. Repeat back important information.

- If you are told who will be interviewing you, be sure to ask for the correct spelling of that person's name so you can do some research. If it's not clear or unstated, ask what the person's title/role is. You need to know whether the person is an HR professional, a department head, a supervisor, or perhaps someone you would work with as a colleague if you were hired.

- If you are talking with an administrative assistant or secretary, don't brush him off. His input counts. One of us (Stan) once had a boss who deliberately left interviewees in the outer office so they would interact with his administrative assistants. Later he would give a lot of weight to their opinions. His view was that people who scorned office staff as "below them" were not team players and were not worth hiring.

- If you receive an e-mail or letter with interview details, you need to be doubly careful that you have spell-checked and eliminated any grammatical errors when replying. Your reply should be concise and professional. Indicate you are very happy to have the opportunity and be sure to include a resume for the interviewer's convenience.

Knowing What's Ahead: Types of Interviews

If there were only one type of interview, preparation would be much easier. Unfortunately, there are a number of variations of the standard interview, each of which requires a somewhat different approach.

The Screening Interview

When you are told that your interview will be with someone from Personnel or HR, it generally means it's a screening interview. Sometimes for positions with a large number of applicants (much more common today in a tough economy), a company's personnel department assumes the task of winnowing down the applicants to a far smaller number. That means this person is looking for any possible reason to eliminate you from the pool. Generally the interview is designed to see whether you really meet the minimal requirements for the position. So, here's the best way to prepare for your interview with what usually turns out to be an innocuous looking "hatchet man."

- Go through the job description very carefully and create two columns on a sheet of paper. In one column list each experience and educational requirement. In the second column match the requirement with what you could bring to the job. As a career changer, you are going to have to carefully consider your transferrable skills and develop a clear explanation as to why they represent equivalent experience. Be sure to consider your volunteer experience as well as job experience and emphasize any training you have. If you don't have any practical work experience in analyzing carbon footprints, but you completed a course covering this information as part of your credential program, be sure to note it.

- Develop your "elevator speech," your concise, one-minute summary of why you believe you are qualified for the position. An HR professional generally will give you a chance during the interview to add anything that you haven't had a chance to say; otherwise, it's perfectly fine for you to bring this up at the close of the interview.

- Express your enthusiasm and also your interest in the industry. Have a few good questions (nothing about salary however) to ask to show your knowledge.

If you follow these steps, the chances are pretty good that you will make it to the second interview, this time hopefully with someone within the department who can hire you.

Telephone Interviews

Sometimes screening interviews are done via telephone. This kind of interview is difficult for applicants because they cannot respond to the body language of the interviewer. Still, here are a few tips to remember to make the phone interview go smoothly.

First, be sure you set up a time when you will have the maximum amount of privacy and quiet (that is, when the kids are at school). You don't want any distractions. Secondly, sit up straight. If you have good posture, your voice will project and you will come across as confident. Finally, have a pad of paper available so you can jot down your thoughts and organize your responses to questions. You want to be sure your answers show that you can think on your feet.

Video Interviews

It is becoming more common now for companies to do an initial interview over the Internet using a webcam. If this turns out to be the case, you will want to dress as if you were going to be interviewed in person...and not just from the waist up. If you "feel" that you are dressed for success, you will perform better. Also keep in mind that any slight movement of your head or body comes across as a major movement during a Web interview.

It is helpful to practice such an interview with a spouse or friend who also has a webcam. Alternatively, have your spouse or friend video you from the waist up and ask you questions. You will want to review the video and critique your body language. (If you own a Macintosh computer, you can use the Photo Booth program to video yourself while you answer questions.)

The Behavioral Interview

The behavioral interview is becoming far more common. Generally HR helps a department in formulating scenario-based questions that are closely related to the job description. The object is to see how you would handle certain job requirements based on how you have handled similar tasks in your previous employment.

When answering behavioral questions, consider the following:

- If you are not sure what the interviewer is driving at or need more time to formulate an answer, you can reiterate the question. Say, "Just to be clear, I understand you want me to explain…."

- Keep in mind that the ideal response usually follows this format: Describe the situation briefly but clearly in terms of what the central issue was. Describe what actions you took. Describe the results.

- Don't panic if you haven't faced the specific situation described in your work life. Think about any other situation, perhaps in your personal life, during college or part-time employment, or during volunteer work that was comparable. If you can't think of anything, you can reply as to how you *would* handle such a situation.

What follows are a couple of examples of the types of questions you can expect in a behavioral interview, along with some guidance as to how to answer them. Keep in mind that this type of interview sometimes is referred to as a "story-telling" interview because your answers generally consist of very concise stories that reinforce your argument that you are well qualified.

> *"In this position, you would have to work with people in several different departments who might have different viewpoints. Can you describe how you handled this type of situation and were able to achieve your objectives?"*

Here the interviewer is really asking for evidence that you are a team player and are also able to take a leadership role. Your answer generally will point to times you have had to work with people from other areas where you had to use your persuasive powers to get things done. Think of a committee you might have served on that produced positive results and emphasize your ability to negotiate, compromise, and inspire.

"Tell me about a difficult problem you faced at work and how you went about solving it."

What the interviewer is looking for here is the process you followed, as well as anything innovative about your solution. So it's important that you provide a logical, step-by-step answer as to how you worked out your solution. Also be sure to quantify the end result if possible.

"Describe the time you faced a stressful situation at work and how you dealt with it."

Clearly the position you are seeking is a stressful one and the interviewer is looking for evidence that you can react calmly and handle problems without falling apart. Follow the three-part format described earlier. Keep in mind that this type of question is common in jobs that involve customer relations and customer support. They are also common in situations where you would be staff support for stressed line managers.

"The person filling this position will be responsible for writing the monthly customer newsletter, creating and giving customer presentations, writing product documentation, and so on. I don't see anything in your resume to indicate you have done these things."

Basic communication skills are the most transferrable of skills. Even if your previous jobs may not have emphasized these skills, you can draw upon your experiences as a volunteer, as well as the occasional opportunities you might have had at work or school. You can assume most interviews will include some kind of communications question and prepare by reviewing your work history ahead of time. Were you asked on occasion to present an idea in committee meetings? Were you ever asked to write a report? What kinds of communications tasks were you required to perform in the classes you took for your certificate? The interviewer is looking for any kind of experience to show you can write and/or speak publicly.

Behavioral-type questions can be tricky, and it's easy to become flustered if you haven't prepared, but they are much easier to deal with if you have done your homework and already have several examples or anecdotes in mind.

The Panel Interview

More and more companies use panel interviews, where interviewers from different departments all interview you at the same time. This is particularly the case if the position you are applying for requires you to work with a number of different departments or agencies. There are several things to keep in mind when preparing for a panel interview:

- When introduced, be sure you are clear as to the name and department for each panelist. Take notes. Also, give each person your undivided attention and make eye contact. There's not a lot of time to relate to each person on a panel, and the introductions are your best chance.

- When you address a panelist's question, keep in mind the perspective of that person's department. Someone from finance is likely to respond well to logic and indications you can be task oriented. A person from marketing, as an example, might be looking for some evidence of your creativity and imagination.

- When answering a question from one panelist, think of a way of answering that addresses that person's question but broadens your answer to include the perspective of other departments as well. For example, if the question is, "How do you work as part of a team?" you might say, "I coordinate my part of the work with others in my department so that the project will be completed on time. I also realize that I need to cooperate and schedule assignments so that other departments will be able to get *their* work done on time." When you say this, look directly at the appropriate panelist.

- Collect business cards from each participant. If one person says they are out of business cards, use the e-mail format of other panelists' business cards when writing a thank-you note. You will want to send a separate thank-you note to each panelist.

The Technical Interview

If your job has a technical component, you might interview with a technical expert, generally someone who would be a colleague of yours should you be hired. Here are some things to keep in mind:

- Look specifically at technical areas described in the job description and review any class material you might have. You can't bluff a fellow techie, so don't even try. If you can't answer a specific question, indicate that it's an area you plan to work on.

- Keep in mind that technical people are not generally professional interviewers. So, you might have to "help" the interviewer by making sure you address your strengths. Be sure to mention technical areas you have covered that might not be apparent from the title on your certificate. If you have been reading trade magazines, be sure to mention which ones you read regularly to show your potential colleague the degree of interest you have in the position and the industry.

- A technical interview is a good place to ask questions about the company and its culture. If you are successful in the interview, there likely will be a follow-up interview with a supervisor who might be less candid about working conditions.

- Because the person interviewing you generally is less experienced in interviewing, he or she is likely to reveal a lot via body language. If you see you are not answering the question to that person's satisfaction, ask if there is something else they are interested in knowing.

- Try to build a positive relationship with the person by agreeing as much as possible. Remember, this person is not just reviewing your technical expertise but also trying to decide if they would like to have you as a colleague. Believe it or not, many times they are wondering if you would be fun and easy to work with. If you come across as too opinionated and inflexible, you're hurting yourself.

- When you write your thank-you note, be sure to indicate that you are looking forward to the possibility of working with this person. Indicate areas of agreement in your note.

The Open-Ended Interview

"Tell me about yourself." This vaguest of questions epitomizes the open-ended interview—one in which you have the most leeway to make your pitch—or to mess it up. The open-ended interview can be the most challenging unless you prepare for it carefully. When asked to tell the interview something about yourself, just remember the following:

- Often the point of this question is to see how well you think on your feet. Rehearse your response to this question ahead of time so your answer is well thought out and concise. Remember, you don't want to relate your life story, but have a well-organized answer with a specific focus.

- Consider a thematic approach, for example, leading with, "I always have been someone who needed a challenge." You then follow up with examples throughout your working life that show you are an innovator and problem solver.

- Another approach is to focus on your career change decision. "A number of things have led me to decide I want to be part of this industry." This gives you the opportunity to showcase your training, skills, technical knowledge, and enthusiasm for the field.

- Be sure to ask for feedback after you've provided an answer to this question. Because it is so broad, it's difficult to know ahead of time specifically what the interviewer is looking for other than to judge how well you can think on your feet. It's perfectly acceptable when you've answered the question to add, "I'm not sure if I've addressed everything you're looking for; is there anything else you'd like me to discuss?"

Following are a few of the more common open-ended questions and strategies for responding to them. Preparing and rehearsing your answers to these questions will give you confidence during the interview.

"What do you view as your greatest strength and your greatest weakness?"

The "strength" answer should be obvious; after all, you know what your best skills are and what the employer is looking for. The "weakness" part of this question is a minefield, however. Some "experts" argue you should present a weakness that is actually a strength ("Sometimes I'm a workaholic."), but that approach is too obvious. A much better approach is to talk about something that *was* a major weakness but now is under control because you recognized the problem and started addressing it. ("I used to have problems prioritizing. I treated everything as equally important and it was impossible to get everything done on time. My manager had me take a class on time management and now I'm much better at organizing my time.")

"Tell me what you enjoyed most about your previous job and what you disliked the most."

This question is a favorite of many interviewers. The interviewer is looking for you to "like" the kinds of tasks you'll be required to perform in the new job. The "dislike" list should minimize what you will be required to do.

As an example, you might indicate you really disliked meetings you had to attend because the manager didn't know how to handle interruptions and kept getting off the agenda.

"I see you've just completed a certificate program. What courses did you enjoy the most and which courses did you not like?"

This is a variation of the previous question. The interviewer is trying to determine how your likes and dislikes about the courses you took correspond to the actual job requirements. In other words, think about this question ahead of time and line up the courses most relevant to the job's description of actual tasks to be preformed. Once again, if you do your homework, this is not a hard question to handle.

"Tell me about a time you were unsuccessful with a work-related project and what you learned from that experience."

This is a tough question. You don't want to paint yourself as a loser, but you can't pretend you have always been perfect. The real heart of this question is the interviewer's desire to learn if you can handle setbacks and learn from them. So, look for an example such as a presentation you gave where your boss felt you missed the mark and what you did on subsequent presentations to improve, or an experience with a customer and what you learned when dealing with customers afterward.

"Give me an example of when you showed initiative and took the lead on a project."

This is an opportunity for you to show your leadership capabilities whether you were a manager or not. The point is to show how you were self-directed. Think of a situation where you took a project from conception to completion. If you haven't had that experience, think of any project that you helped drive to completion. It might even be a pet project that you were told to work on during your spare time. The point to emphasize is how you managed to get colleagues to cooperate with you even if you weren't their supervisor.

"What is your long-term career objective?"

Because you are a career changer, this is a chance for you to show the interviewer that you know something about the industry and a possible career track. You can use a variety of resources to prepare for this question, including the BLS's career guides or a detailed study of the jobs section of the company that is interviewing you. What you want to do is look at the experience and education requirements for the position you are applying for as well as similar positions that require slightly more experience or education. As an example, you might be applying for an energy auditor position. You find that there are also descriptions of senior energy auditors and even energy auditing managers. You can lay out a five-to-ten-year career plan that is consistent with the job descriptions of the company that will be interviewing you. Leave the interviewer with the impression that you have long-range plans to stay with the company should it hire you.

> **Painter's Tip:** If you plan to work toward a specific certification after you gain a bit more experience, then say so. It shows you are serious about this career. Who knows, the company may even have the means to help you pay for it.

"What is your greatest achievement?"

Give a specific illustration from your previous or current job where you saved the company money or helped increase profits. If you just graduated, try to find some accomplishment from school, part-time jobs, or extracurricular activities. Be sure to quantify the results.

"Why should we hire you?"

In many ways, this is the question interviewers are always asking; they just usually aren't so blunt about it. Still, if you get asked this directly, it's an open invitation to hit them with your best skills and most relevant experience. Highlight your background based on the company's current needs. Recap your qualifications by using words from the job description. If you don't have much experience, talk about how your education and training prepared you for this job.

Following are a few more common questions and sample responses, just to give you an idea of what approach you might take.

"Why have you been out of work for so long?"

Answer: "I spent some time re-evaluating my past experience and the current job market to see what direction I wanted to take. I had some job offers but I'm not looking for just a 'job.' I'm looking for a career."

"What do you know about our company? Why do you want to work here?"

Answer: Use your research findings to answer this question. For example, "Your company is a leader in the _____ field and you are growing." Or, "Your company has superior products (name them) and excellent customer service."

"Why do you want to make a career change now?"

Answer: "I've been in my present company for several years and new opportunities are limited. I've done a lot of research and green jobs are in high demand. I've looked at my transferable skills and I have a lot to offer from previous jobs that apply to your company (give examples). Plus I'm taking classes in green technology to upgrade my skills."

Finally, keep the following in mind when handling these and other open-ended questions, particularly about previous jobs you have had:

- Never outright lie. If the open-ended question is about how well you got along with your previous supervisors, it is far better to just cast the best light on the situation: "He didn't provide much guidance, but I took the opportunity to develop several initiatives of my own." You might indicate that there are several former colleagues who would provide a much more accurate perspective on your work history at that company than your former supervisor.

- Be honest, but try to figure out what the interviewer is looking for. If you are asked about what you look for in a good supervisor, for example, be honest to a point but be sure to describe a supervisor's qualities that enhance *your* image. In other words, you certainly want a supervisor who is fair, but you probably also want one who allows you to show initiative even if that means being accountable. You also probably look for a supervisor who wants to work with you on a career development plan to help you grow with the company. Such an answer shows you are loyal and have initiative.

- Don't answer the question about salary history directly. If you are asked for your salary history, try to be vague. You don't want to limit yourself to a lower salary even though this new job might have greater responsibilities. On the other hand, since you are changing careers, you might be taking a salary cut and you don't want the interviewer to think you would not be happy with the lower salary. We'll cover salary discussions at more length later in the chapter.

THERE IS SUCH A THING AS A BAD QUESTION

Questions *you* shouldn't ask...

Never ask any questions about salary, overtime pay, paid vacations, holidays, or sick time (until hired). It's not about what the job has to offer you (although they *should* try to sell you on the company). It's all about what you have to offer the company to make them successful.

Questions *they* shouldn't ask...

During an interview you may be asked some questions that are considered illegal and shouldn't be asked (such as questions related to age, sex, race, religion, natural origin, marital status, or number of kids). You will need to stop and think before choosing to answer. How uncomfortable has the question made you feel? Does the interviewer seem unaware that the question is illegal? Will the interviewer be your boss?

If you decide to answer, be succinct and try to redirect the conversation back to your skills and abilities. For example, if asked about your age, you might reply, "I'm in my forties and I have a lot of experience in the area your company is looking for." If you're not sure you want to answer, ask for clarification of how the question relates to your qualifications for the job. You might answer if there is a reasonable explanation. But if there is no justification for the question, you might say you don't see the relationship between the question and your qualifications for the job and you prefer not to answer.

The Badly Managed Interview

There is one more type of interview you should be aware of, though we hope you never experience it yourself.

One advantage of having a person from human resources conducting an interview is that it generally is done professionally. The major disadvantage, however, is that the HR person has no power to hire, only the power to eliminate you from the pile of applicants. A department manager or supervisor, on the other hand, likely lacks as much interviewing experience, but he or she does have the power to hire you.

Unfortunately that lack of interview experience can lead to a miserable experience. It may be the case that you interview with someone who has no idea what he or she is doing. If so, then it is your responsibility to make the interview a success by giving the managers or supervisors what they are looking for (even if they don't know how to ask), namely,

- They want someone who matches up with the job description they probably helped write, so be sure to cover those points in your discussion even if you have to initiate that conversation.

- They want someone who is enthusiastic.

- They want someone who can help the company grow. If you have done your research, you know about some company initiatives. Indicate how you could help with some of them.

- They want someone who requires little effort to bring up to speed. Be sure to point out examples of where you have taken the initiative to learn material as well as your performance in your certificate classes if they merit discussion.

- They want someone who is little trouble to manage; talk about how well you can take direction and then use your own initiative to complete a task.

- They want someone who will remain with the company. It's time-consuming and expensive to keep replacing people. Talk about your career goals and how you would like to grow within the company.

- Be sure your questions about the company reflect your enthusiasm and interest. Well-thought-out questions will help your interviewer see that you are serious about working for that company and that you are industry-savvy even though you are changing careers.

- Bring up the career change issue even if the interviewer doesn't. Explain why you are making this change and how many of the skills you developed in your previous career are transferrable. It's important to address this "elephant in the room" because this type of interviewer might have reservations about that career change but not know how to frame the question.

- Finally, be sure to bring up your talking points and conclude with a brief summary of why you think you'd be a good match for the position. Some inexperienced interviewers tend to ramble rather than direct enough questions to you.

How to Prepare for the Interview

There are a number of steps to take when preparing for an interview, regardless of what type it is. Let's go through them one-by-one.

Research the Industry

The company you are interviewing with is impacted by what happens in that industry and certainly by the actions of major competitors. Industry research resources are expensive, however, so you will need to take advantage of public libraries, college libraries or career centers, and any online resources. Following are a few sources of industry information:

- **Standard & Poor's Industry Surveys [via S&P Net Advantage]:** This resource includes a basic section that describes an industry and the leading players as well as the current analysis that covers the latest industry developments.

- **Thompson One Banker:** A database of industry overviews by Wall Street analysts.

- **ipl2:** A site sponsored by Drexel University and Florida State University (www.ipl.org). Under "Special Collections" is an "Associations" category that you can use to search through hundreds of professional associations and identify the key ones associated with the industry you are researching. Links to these associations are provided.

- **AllBusiness (www.allbusiness.com):** This site allows free searching through seven million articles in 1,500 professional journals. Searching on a term such as "solar energy" results in several articles on that industry.

- **The Department of Labor Career Guides (www.bls.gov/oco/cg/):** This resource can provide you with key information on an industry's growth rate, typical salary ranges, and prospects for employment.

Research the Employer

In Chapter 6 we discussed how to best research the companies that you are interested in, but here are a few more tips. For starters, you should know that local libraries usually have access to databases and online business directories that you can use to learn more about a company. Ask a librarian to assist you.

Before any interview, be sure to browse the company's own website. Remember to look at the "News" section, as well as the websites of its major competitors. Read up on trade magazine articles that include mentions of the company. Often there also will be links to free industry analyst reports, which are goldmines when it comes to finding competitive information. You can learn a company's strengths and its weaknesses by studying such reports.

> **Painter's Tip:** One technique for researching a company is to study the jobs it advertises on its website. Look for patterns. For example, if the company is advertising for people who speak Mandarin, then it is likely there's a planned expansion into China. Doing this kind of homework will result in some great questions you can ask during your interview.

Following are a few more resources you can use to learn more about employers:

- **The Wall Street Transcript (www.twst.com):** This website allows you to search for the full text of speeches and question-and-answer sessions a company's CEO has with wall street analysts. While there is a fee for a transcript, it is invaluable to know what a company's CEO is saying about the company's strategy, the company's major competitors, new product plans, and so on.

- **The SEC Edgar Website (www.sec.gov/edgar.shtml):** This jewel allows you to retrieve financial documents companies must submit to the SEC.

- **Hoovers (www.hoovers.com):** This is a fee-based site with only partial information available free. Most libraries subscribe to Hoovers, so it's worth a visit to your local library. Hoovers is particularly valuable for learning about private companies.

- **Vault (www.vault.com/wps/portal/usa):** This website offers company profiles including salary information.

Research the Job

It's worth the time to take the job title you have applied for and search for similar positions at competitor companies. What you are looking for are any significant differences in job descriptions. If there are certain tasks that are listed in job descriptions at competitor companies but not in your job's description, then note the differences. Asking about these tasks shows that you have some understanding of the specific job. It makes you look professional and motivated.

Research the Interviewer

Often you will be told ahead of time the name of the person who will be interviewing you. It's important, particularly if the person is in a line position and not in HR, that you research his or her background. There are several reasons to do so:

- You can learn what this person's specific interests are and brush up on those areas before the interview.

- You can learn where the person went to school. You might very well share a similar background that will help break the ice.

- You can learn if the person is active in any trade association initiatives. If they are, you can be sure to ask about them. The interviewer will be surprised and flattered that you even know about his or her involvement.

Using Google with quotations around the person's full name is a good way to begin. If the person is an executive, the company's website often will have a brief biography. You might find press releases where the interviewer is quoted. If you know which product initiatives he is involved in, you can ask questions about them and show that you are familiar with the company.

You should also have a list of major trade magazines for your particular industry. These magazines are all online and offer search engines. It's worth spending some time on these websites searching for news stories that mention your interviewer. In the process, you will also learn a lot more about both the company and the industry.

Finally, you can search social networking sites such as LinkedIn and Facebook. These sites can provide you with personal information that could point you to areas of mutual interest. If your interviewer is a girl's soccer coach or active in the Boy Scouts or a particular religious organization, there is always the potential of a match with your background. You can bring up some of these volunteer activities that you are active in without mentioning your online reconnaissance. Remember, it is natural for people to like people who seem more like themselves.

Painter's Tip: If all this personal research sounds like cheating, keep in mind that employers will often go to personal websites to learn more about *you*. That's an excellent reason to pull down any off-color jokes or photos you might have up on your own website.

Interview Yourself

One technique that Stan has used that has always worked is to practice interviewing himself before a big interview. There is a process to this:

- No one knows your strengths and weakness and gaps in your resume better than you do, so write down the very hardest questions you could possibly be asked, the ones that you know would make you squirm. If you have been fired, for example, assume that you'll be asked about it. The point is to make the questions so difficult that the real interview will seem much easier.

- Practice asking the questions and then answer them. Look at yourself in a mirror or record yourself if possible. At first you might have to look at notes, but after several iterations you should be able to answer these questions without them.

- Continue to practice asking and answering these questions. You can even practice in your car while driving to an interview. After a while you'll begin to feel comfortable answering virtually any question.

Painter's Tip: Find someone to help you rehearse the interview. This should be someone you feel comfortable with, who can be objective and knows you well, so if you leave something out—such as an important accomplishment—they can remind you.

Step back and analyze your performance. Work on correcting your weaknesses, such as speaking too fast; talking too loudly or too softly; offering a weak handshake; or nervous habits like tapping your pen, shaking your leg, drumming your fingers, or rocking in your chair. Most people are a little nervous in an interview, and the employer knows that. He or she will try to help you feel comfortable by conducting the interview in a relaxed, conversational way.

Make a Good Impression

There are a number of things that you need to do to ensure that you don't shoot yourself in the foot before you even open your mouth at the interview.

- Prepare your body for an interview like it was an athletic event or a final exam: You want to peak at the time of the interview. That means ensuring that you have a good night's sleep. It also means eating a breakfast or lunch loaded with protein and complex carbohydrates so that you will have energy.

- Dress with your industry in mind. Anything that sets you apart from the norm and suggests a lifestyle that might not mesh with that of the interviewer is not acceptable. That means muted colored nails for women, no flashy jewelry, and no nose rings. Acceptable attire for most industries is conservative, so suits for men and a suit or dress and jacket for women is a safe choice. It is better to be overdressed than too casual.

- Have several interviewing outfits available because you may be called back for a second, third, and even fourth interview. Your clothes should be clean and ironed and your shoes polished. Hair should be clean and modernly styled. Avoid excessive make-up. If possible, cover any tattoos.

- Hands need to be clean and fingernails trimmed neatly. Interviewers *will* notice your hands. They will want to shake, after all.

- Use a non-perfumed deodorant and watch what you eat for at least a couple of days before the interview. Avoid garlic and other food items that might affect your breath and body odor. Also eliminate the possibility that you might have bad breath by brushing before leaving for the interview. Use breath mints just beforehand.

- It's important to *feel* that you look good. If you can afford it, buy a new interviewing outfit. A new dress, a new shirt and tie, and even new shoes can make you feel better about yourself.

- It's better to use a great-smelling soap or shampoo than to load up on cologne or perfume. Some people are allergic to perfumes, and you don't want to annoy anyone. What might seem to be a light spray to you might overwhelm someone else.

- Bring a brush and comb with you. Arrive early and use a restroom to ensure that your hair looks nice. Make sure a collar is not turned up or a slip showing.

- Bring a professional-looking attaché case with you to hold copies of your resume as well as a nice-looking pen that works, a pad of paper, and any examples of your work. You want everything—including your writing accessories—to suggest that you are a professional.

Don't Neglect the Details

The last thing in the world you want to happen is to arrive late for your big interview or to arrive on time but flustered. You want to eliminate as many variables as you can when it comes to doing well on the interview, so do the following:

- When you are invited for an interview, usually you will be given the address as well as key details such as who to ask for and which gate to enter. Make multiple copies of this information and place one copy in your attaché case immediately.

- Use MapQuest or other GPS sites to determine specifically which route to take to the interview location. If you have time, try actually driving there ahead of time to see if there is anything along the route that could confuse you.

- Plan on arriving at the parking lot around 30 minutes early. You will want a little time to review your notes, as well as go to a restroom and freshen up. If it helps you to relax, bring a book or magazine and read for a few minutes in your car before going in. You should not arrive to the interview itself more than 15 minutes early.

- One of the secrets of successful athletes is to visualize themselves succeeding. Imagine yourself shaking hands at the end of the interview and learning that you likely will be called back.

- Don't fidget. Look at the magazines or company literature in the waiting room.

- Introduce yourself to the receptionist and be pleasant. Indicate who you are scheduled to talk with. Don't treat the receptionist as a hired servant or permanent member of the underclass. Remember, he or she is already working for the company and you are not.

Acing the Interview

The following sections look specifically at how to handle the actual interview, from the opening handshake to the closing one—and all the nuances in between.

Greet the Interviewer

When the time comes, greet your interviewer warmly. Shake hands solidly but don't try to win the contest for the strongest grip. If you have been told that you have clammy hands, be sure you wipe them off as inconspicuously as possible.

Look the interviewer directly in the eye during the greeting. You might not even realize that many people look down when greeting someone new out of shyness. That should not be you. If you are not sure of how to pronounce the interviewer's name or how to spell it, be sure to ask. After you're in the office, you can ask for a card if one is not offered.

Get Off to a Good Start

It's an unfortunate truth that people often decide whether or not they like someone in the first couple of minutes. You want to make sure you get off to a good start with your interviewer. That means you smile when you meet them and let them know how excited you are about the opportunity to interview for the position. Often the interviewer will start off with small talk. Try to find points of interest in these first few minutes—something you and the interviewer have in common—like an interest in sports or a shared hobby.

Maintain a 50/50 Split

The ideal interview consists of each participant talking around 50 percent of the time. It's not an absolute rule, but certainly you don't want the interviewer to go into an hour-long monologue; conversely, you don't want to just keep talking because you're nervous. A professional interviewer will keep the interview balanced. If you see that the interviewer is not skilled and is drifting, you can bring the conversation back to the position and begin talking about what you could bring to it. In other words, you might have to take some control.

ADAPT TO YOUR INTERVIEWER'S STYLE

Managers who interview job candidates usually fall into four basic types:

- **The "All-Business" Interviewer:** Direct, hard-nosed, and in a rush, they want to know what you've accomplished. Keep your answers brief, stick to the facts, and use numbers and specific data.

- **The "Good Guy" Interviewer:** Warm, friendly, and likable. Wants to know if you will fit in with the group. Emphasize that you're a "team player" and use "we" instead of "I."

- **The "Abstract" Interviewer:** Wants to know how you think, how you perform tasks, how you approach theoretical problems. Be logical, methodical, clear, and concise in your answers.

- **The "Indecisive" Interviewer:** Disorganized, unfocused, and uncomfortable making decisions. This interviewer would rather talk about himself. Let him talk to get comfortable and respond with enthusiasm and interest.

Counter Objections

Think of your interview as a sales pitch. Occasionally the interviewer, much like a potential customer, will raise objections. An objection is any reason why you might not be the right person for the job. Don't get flustered. It is much better to have that objection aired than to have it unasked and therefore unanswered.

During your preparation for this interview you should list possible objections. They might include your lack of experience in the industry, the fact you likely would be taking a pay cut, and so on. Rehearse how you would answer these objections well ahead of time so that you can counter each objection professionally.

As an example, let's assume that the interviewer raises the objection that because you are a career changer, you don't have as much experience as other people applying for the job. Your answer might point to the fact that much of your previous job experience and skills are directly transferrable to this position. You might point out that because your training is so recent, you are more up-to-speed on the latest technology than people who have been in the field a bit longer. You might also respond how quickly you are able to pick up new skills and give examples. Whatever your answer to this particular objection, the key is to have it prepared and rehearsed well ahead of time.

The worst thing is for the interviewer to harbor some serious reservations about you but not give you the chance to defend yourself. One way to handle this situation is to bring up certain things on your resume that *might* raise some objections and then counter them preemptively. As an example, you might say something like this: "We haven't really talked about the fact that I've made a major career change. I think it's actually a plus for [company] because I'm coming to this new career filled with enthusiasm and also having been exposed to some of the very latest technology." You then can go into some details. The point is that once you air this objection, the interviewer might come back with further questions. Once you have addressed these objections and the interviewer says there are no follow-up questions, you've gone a long way toward ensuring your success.

Handle Other Difficult Questions with Confidence

There are some questions that you just know are going to be potential roadblocks to your getting the job. You should be prepared to address these if they apply to you.

- **"Why did you change careers?"** This should not be a difficult question, but it is for some people. Are you looking for greater job satisfaction? Do you want to feel you are contributing to a making the planet greener? Think hard about this question ahead of time and have an answer that contrasts what you experienced in your previous career and what you would hope to find in your new career. Make sure it's not just about the money.

- **"I see on your application you were convicted of a crime."** You can't lie about something like this. Work up an answer ahead of time that is sure to explain that you made a huge mistake and that you learned from it. Don't fail to take responsibility. If there are mitigating circumstances, you can mention them first but then take responsibility and explain what you have learned the hard way. People are much more likely to give a second chance to someone who takes responsibility for their own mistakes rather than simply blames others.

- **"It looks like you were fired or laid-off."** If you were part of a large layoff, quantify it to make it seem less personal. If you were offered another job but couldn't accept it, be sure to bring that fact up because it makes you less expendable. If you were fired, don't simply lambaste your old boss because the person interviewing you might assume you will not accept personal responsibility and will blame your *next* firing on your *next* boss. It's best to point to the fact that you differed on policy or grew apart because of certain specific conditions rather than make it seem like a personality conflict. You don't want to come across as difficult.

- **"It looks like you've done a lot of job hopping. Why?"** Let's face it. At one time a job was virtually a lifetime contract. Obviously that's not the case today. It is not the stigma it used to be for someone's resume to show a lot of different jobs in a relatively short time, but it still raises red flags. Why? The answer is that no company wants invest time and money only to see that person leave in a relatively short time. So, if you have been a job hopper, you have to be prepared to handle that question when it arises. Can you point to something at each position that you found lacking? Did you feel you weren't able to utilize some of the skills you had? The challenge is to build a compelling "story" that shows that your several different jobs have led up to this particular job and that this job provides you with the opportunity to use all your skills and to grow.

Painter's Tip: Don't focus on the inadequacies of the companies you worked for. If you have nothing but bad things to say about your former employers, most interviewers will write you off as a chronic malcontent who will never be satisfied and they won't hire you.

Ask Questions

Usually a professional interviewer will ask you if you have any questions about the company or about the position. The answer should always be "yes." Here are a few good questions to get you started, though you should certainly think of several more on your own.

- Is there anything we haven't talked about that you would like to ask me?
- How will your new [initiative or product offering] impact this position?
- Does the company offer career development plans?
- The company seems to be advertising for people in the area of [new area]. How would that impact my position?

- What is the typical career path for people with this position?
- Does the company promote from within?

Remember that asking intelligent, well-informed questions shows that you have done your research, that you are knowledgeable about the industry, and that you are eager to learn more.

> **Painter's Tip:** Remember, now is not the time to ask about salary or benefits. Wait until you are offered the job. You also shouldn't ask about other candidates; it's just not polite.

Summarize Your Qualifications

Before you go to your interview, you need to have worked out a very good summary of your strengths and the reasons why you think you are qualified for the position. Generally your argument will lead with a thematic statement, such as, "I believe there are a number of reasons why I would make an excellent [job title] for [the company]," followed by your three most important reasons.

As a career changer, be sure to work in your enthusiasm as well as your recent training. If your research has shown that the company plans to grow in certain areas, link your experience and training to those areas to show why you would be a real asset.

Practice giving this summary while looking into a mirror. Work on good eye contact and a natural speech pattern. Though you want to *be* well rehearsed, you don't want to *sound* rehearsed. If you practice enough, you will be able to talk naturally and make it appear that you are thinking on your feet rather than reciting a canned speech.

Ask About Next Steps

It is perfectly acceptable as an interview winds down for you to ask about "next steps" as well as a likely timeline. What you really want to know is whether or not the process includes another interview and what the timeline is for setting up the next interview. Usually the interviewer will say something like, "Well, it's going to take us a while to get through this round of interviews. We expect to meet next week to discuss them and then we plan to schedule interviews with our finalists. It's a busy time, however, so don't panic if you don't hear from us for a while."

What the interviewer is really saying is that if you don't hear from the company within the next couple of weeks, you probably didn't make the cut. They would prefer that you don't hound them. Still, you can wait two weeks and then write or phone to ask about how things are progressing. Calling shows you really are interested in the position. Don't be a pest though. Remember that even if you don't get this particular job, there might be others in the near future that do open up, and you want them to think of you in a positive way.

HOW LONG IS THIS GOING TO TAKE?

Unfortunately for most jobs the initial interview is only the first step toward getting the job. You may have to navigate your way through several interviews before being hired:

The telephone interview: This is generally a screening interview conducted by someone in the HR department. Your entire objective is to prove you should go on to the next level by meeting or exceeding the minimum requirements.

The first interview: Here's your chance to go from being on the "long list" to being on the "short list." Your objective is to show why you are a much better choice than most of the others being interviewed so that you can get on a list of three or so finalists. If you believe you lack some of the experience and education of your competitors, you'll have to wow them with your potential and your enthusiasm.

The second interview: This interview often includes the person who will be your supervisor. If you do well on this interview, the journey may still not be complete, but you're close to the top. Hopefully you have reviewed your previous interview(s) with the company and you know topics where you didn't seem to satisfy the earlier interviewer(s). Here's your chance to work in additional points you might have forgotten.

The final interview: Depending on the level of the position, this interview could be with future colleagues or with your boss' boss. If it's with future colleagues, then essentially your supervisor is saying that he or she thinks you're very well qualified and is asking for his employees' opinion. It's important that you make an effort to relate to these interviewers. If you are scheduled for an interview with your boss's superior, it's generally just a pro forma meeting for a final sign-off. If you are polite and professional, you will get the job after this interview assuming your references check out.

Handle the Salary Question

There's an old saying that the person who brings up the topic of salary first loses. There's some truth to that. During a screening interview or the first of a series of interviews, your answer to the salary question can only do you harm. Either you will come in at a salary level that is so high that you are dismissed from further consideration or you might come up with a salary figure that is so low that the interviewer might consider you below the level of person they are seeking or, conversely, hire you at that figure and make it impossible for you to ever reach the appropriate level for the position.

So, initially, you should indicate that your salary is negotiable based on the duties. If they press you, ask what the range is for the position and indicate that you were thinking of a salary close to the top of that range.

Now let's assume that you have navigated through the obstacle course and have been offered the position. Presumably you have done some research and know the general salary range in advance. If the salary range the interviewer has revealed is fair, shoot for the high end of it so you can be comparably paid with your colleagues. If your research reveals that the salary range offered is below the industry norm, then indicate the minimum salary that you require. You can then point to your own research to show that it is appropriate for someone with your background. Generally company managers don't reveal all their cards initially so there might be some room for the company to increase its offer.

If you run into a wall and yet you still want the job, then indicate that the salary is acceptable *if* the company can offer an early salary review. Then just do a good job from the start and you are likely to get your raise.

Handle Requests for References

Let's assume that the interviewer indicates he or she would like to talk with some references. This is what *you* need to do:

- Talk with the references *before* the interviewer does. If you are asked at the end of the interview, indicate you have the contact information at home and will call or e-mail the information as soon as possible.

- Tell each of your references how you described your relationship with them in the interview. Indicate what specifically they can tell the interviewer that might prove helpful. We're not suggesting you tell the references to lie. Just ask them to emphasize certain skills you demonstrated or describe situations where you performed well.

- If you have had a bad relationship with a supervisor, don't use that person. Use a colleague or other manager with whom you worked and explain to them why you didn't use your supervisor. Presumably they can put the best light on a bad situation.
- You don't want to overuse your references. You shouldn't provide them unless you are told you are a finalist for a position.

After the Interview

There are a number of things you should do after the interview:

- While everything is fresh in your mind, do a post-mortem of your interview. Jot down the questions that gave you the most trouble. Also indicate any objections the interviewer had that you couldn't completely satisfy. You will want to review these questions and work on your answers before your next interview.
- Don't be overly aggressive. If you don't hear back from the company within the proscribed time the interviewer indicated, it's appropriate to call or e-mail the interviewer. Indicate you wanted to check on the progress of the process. Often you will be told that no decision had been made yet.
- If you are told the position has been filled, ask if the interviewer would be candid and tell you areas that you should work on in order to do better on the next interview.
- Tell the interviewer that you still are very much interested in the company and that you would like to be considered if any other positions open up.

And of course you should send the appropriate thank-you notes. Sending notes on quality stationary makes a good impression. You can also send a thank-you by e-mail, but follow it up with a handwritten note as well.

The thank-you note should

- Be typed or handwritten on quality white or cream-colored paper.
- Be simple and brief.
- Express your appreciation for the interviewer's time.
- Show enthusiasm for the job.
- Ask for the job and assure the interviewer you can do it.

Most thank-you notes follow the same general format:

- An opening paragraph stating that it was a pleasure to meet with the interviewer and thanking him or her for the important information that was shared.

- A second paragraph that either reiterates your skills and qualifications that you know the employer is looking for or clarifies any information that you feel is relevant to the position.

- A closing paragraph that again thanks the interviewer for his or her time and consideration. You can restate your interest in the position and that you are available for any follow-up.

Following is a sample thank-you note:

John Brown
Senior Environmental Engineer
ABC Excavating Company
321 Professional Way
Los Angeles, CA 92832

Dear Mr. Brown:

It was a pleasure to visit you today and to meet the members of your staff while interviewing for the Junior Environmental Engineer position. I was pleased with the opportunity to get a closer look at ABC Excavating and to hear of the many green projects being undertaken.

I think I would be a valuable addition to your company. My recent schooling and internship have given me up-to-date, hands-on experience in project management and a chance to use the latest technology and statistical methods. My previous five years working at James Smith Construction gave me the experience in grading, design, and environmental safety that you are looking for.

I am very interested in joining ABC. My best friend, Sam Black, has been there as a Project Coordinator for over a year and he tells me it is a great company to work for. Thank you again for your time and consideration. I am available for any follow-up information that you might need and can be reached at (818) 354-9785. I look forward to hearing from you soon.

Sincerely,

(Your name)

So now you know what to expect from the interview that will transition you into your new "green" career. You can go into your interview with a confident, enthusiastic attitude knowing you are prepared. If you project that you can do the job, want the job, and are excited about the opportunity, you should have no problem reaching your goals and successfully repainting your career.

CHAPTER 10

Preparing for Your Green Career—Short-Term Training Opportunities

This chapter introduces you to the many ways you can get the training and certification you need to paint yourself green. The emphasis in this book is on making a career transition as quickly and painlessly as possible. That means obtaining the minimum training that validates your expertise and provides you with a certificate to pass the initial screening for a green position.

Because of this, we have not included four-year degree programs unless those universities also offer much shorter certificate programs. Many of the most attractive certificates are being offered by community colleges or by educational organizations online. Remember that even though an associate degree requires two years of study, many community colleges offer certificate programs lasting only a year.

> **Painter's Tip:** If you have lots of other obligations, keep distance education in mind. An online credential from a four-year accredited university will serve you just as well, and you won't have to spend time on campus, away from your family and current job.

Colleges and nonprofit organizations are adding new green certificate programs all the time. We've made an effort to make this chapter as complete as possible, but don't be discouraged if you don't find the perfect program listed. If you spend some time searching the Web, you're likely to find a new program that is just right for you. Finally, feel free to skip ahead to the sections that match your specific career interests—or just go to the table at the end of the chapter and start researching your options.

FOR THOSE WHO ARE GREEN ALREADY

Because the majority of readers will not have prior green job experience, there are many certificate programs that we don't address—programs designed for people already immersed in a green industry. One example is the program offered by the Association of Energy Engineers (www. Aeecenter.org). This organization offers certification for energy engineers, carbon managers, and even an energy manager in training.

Unfortunately even the latter certificate requires a minimum of two years' experience working in energy management. So, these are great credentials to add to your resume after you have some green job experience. They can become part of a long-term career plan.

The Green Auto Industry

The Midwest prospered when Detroit was the global center of the auto industry; it suffered proportionately as the American auto industry fell on hard times. The good news is that the very areas of the country devastated by consumer's rejection of gas guzzlers is poised to make a comeback with a variety of technologies ranging from hybrids to fuel cells to hydrogen-fueled cars. As Table 10.1 (shown later in this chapter) reveals, much of the certificate training required to become part of this new auto industry is centered in the Midwest, particular in Michigan. Four-year colleges in Michigan such as the University of Michigan, Central Michigan University, Ferris State University, and Western Michigan University offer full-blown automotive engineering degree programs. A consortium of community colleges in Southern California also offers some very compelling certificate programs in new automobile technology.

Remember that this type of training is not just beneficial to people who want to design green cars. These programs will also prove useful for fleet managers, salespeople, and even the marketing personnel who design campaigns for green cars. Mechanics trained in new green technology will be needed, as will people to train employees, write technical manuals, write press releases, and so on.

The certificate programs for advanced automotive technology are remarkably similar throughout the country. The following abbreviated descriptions from Lansing Community College's 2010 course catalog will give you an idea of what you could learn in such a program.

Electric/Fuel Cell Technology

This course is designed to help prepare the student to enter the automotive repair and service industry in the area of alternative fuels and advanced technology vehicles. It is an intensive study of vehicle electric and fuel cell theory, application, installation, diagnosis, service, and safety regulations.

Hybrid Fuel Technology

This course covers the fundamentals of hybrid vehicle technology. The course is intended to give the student an understanding of the types of hybrid vehicles, hybrid vehicle components, how hybrid vehicles operate, and basic service procedures; this will enable the student to obtain employment as an advanced technology vehicle technician.

Fuel Cell and Hydrogen Technology

This course will focus on fuel cell conversion devices and other hydrogen-based technologies. The history of hydrogen and fuel cell technologies, their application, instrumentation, specifications, codes, system designs, and materials will be covered. Basic thermodynamics and heat/mass transfer technology will be discussed. Specific licensing, permits, and safety issues will be covered.

FOR BIOFUEL TRAINING, THINK IOWA

There's a reason political candidates always talk about ethanol when they are campaigning in Iowa. This state is the center of biofuel and biomass training at places like Des Moines Area Community College and Iowa Lakes Community College. There are also training facilities available in Minnesota and Wisconsin as well as in North Carolina. Remember that many green careers are dependent on location. Although distance learning options are often available, you may have to relocate eventually to chase your dream green career.

Green Buildings and Construction

One way to break into the green construction industry is to earn a LEED (Leadership in Energy and Environmental Design) Green Associate certificate. The Green Building Certification Institute lists the requirements as follows:

Candidates must have experience in the form of:

EITHER documented involvement on a project registered or certified for LEED

OR employment (or previous employment) in a sustainable field of work

OR engagement in (or completion of) an education program that addresses green building principles.

For most readers the third option is the most likely scenario. You will first need to take some classes in green construction. In addition, to maintain this LEED credential, you'll need to take 15 units of continuing education every two years. You can learn more information at the Green Building Certification Institute website: www.gbci.org.

The Building Performance Institute (BPI) is a non-profit organization that develops technical standards for home performance and weatherization retrofit work as well as training programs that are offered nationally by its affiliates. The following certificates are currently available, though by the time you read this there may be more:

- **Building Analyst:** Training beyond an energy audit to perform comprehensive, whole-home assessments, identify problems at the root cause, and prescribe and prioritize solutions based on building science.

- **Envelope:** Training to quantify performance and prescribe improvements to help tighten the building envelope (shell); stop uncontrolled air leakage, and optimize comfort, durability, and HV/AC performance.

- **Residential Building Envelope Accessible Areas Air Leakage Control Installer:** Training to implement measures to tighten the building envelope to reduce energy loss from air leakage and also reduce pollutants and allergens through air migration. There is also training to improve thermal comfort and energy efficiency through the proper installation of dense-pack insulation materials.

- **Residential Building Envelope Whole House Air Leakage Control Crew Chief:** Training to provide supervision, guidance, and quality control to teams in the field working on controlling air migration through the building envelope, and also on the proper installation of dense-pack insulation materials.

- **Manufactured Housing:** Training to apply house-as-a-system fundamentals to the specific needs particular to the various types of housing technologies.

- **Heating:** Training to optimize the performance of heating equipment to help save energy and ensure occupant comfort, health, and safety.

- **Air Conditioning and Heat Pump:** Training to understand the role of these systems within the whole home and how to diagnose and correct problems properly to achieve peak performance.

- **Multifamily:** Training to apply building-as-a-system fundamentals to diagnose problems and improve the performance of larger, more complex residential structures.

Green Real Estate

Green Real Estate Education (www.greenrealestateeducation.com) offers a series of green building courses (the Real Estate Environmental and Energy Education Certification Series) that leads to a Green Certified Real Estate Professional certificate. The Green Leadership (GL) Certification provides an introduction to energy efficiency, sustainability, and green building relating to all real estate professions including real estate professionals, appraisers, inspectors and mortgage professionals, handymen, plumbers, electricians, and others. The company offers certifications for building inspectors and mortgage professionals and is planning to offer additional real estate certifications, including a green design and material certification, renewable energy certification, green residential specialist, and green commercial specialist.

Ecobroker (www.ecobroker.com) offers a three-course program for people who have Realtor licenses to become certified as ecobrokers. The courses can be taken online. For those readers who currently are Realtors but would like to become "green" Realtors, here are the three courses that must be completed within six months:

- The EcoBroker Environmental Advantage course provides resources to evaluate and improve indoor air quality and water quality for health and comfort. The course also provides information on the "health and savings benefits of green buildings."

- The EcoBroker Energy Advantage course explains energy-saving home features and sustainable energy options such as solar power. It also explains how to use energy savings and green financing tools.

- The EcoBroker Green Market Advantage course explains how to reach clients who consider themselves green-minded as well as how to reach new markets and "gain business with clients looking for green expertise in selling and buying properties with green features."

Solar Installation

The North American Board of Certified Energy Practitioners (NABCEP) has an entry-level program that targets people who want to get into the solar field. It offers an NABCEP PV (photovoltaic) Entry Level Exam so that people can demonstrate that they have achieved a basic knowledge of the fundamental principles of the application, design, installation, and operation of grid-tied and stand-alone PV Systems.

There are a number of NAPCEP PV Entry Level Exam providers. The organization's website has a map so that students can locate the closest training facility (www.nabcep.org). Students completing the coursework successfully are eligible to take the PV Entry Level Exam. Note: Passing this exam does *not* mean that a student is qualified to install PV systems; it means that a student has a good understanding of basic terms and operational aspects of a PV system and thus is more likely to be hired into a training position.

Wind Energy

As noted in Chapter 4, the majority of wind energy jobs will be in states where wind is an available resource. One obvious example is Texas. Midland, Texas, is the home of Midland College, which offers a program in energy technology that prepares graduates for jobs as field, installation, operation, and maintenance technicians.

The *best* single source of information on training for wind technology is the free database offered by the American Wind Energy Association. It lists training opportunities at technical schools, community colleges, and four-year schools. You can search by state and by type of program (that is, certificate, associate degree). Check it out at www.awea2.org.

Distance Learning

An increasing number of interesting certificate programs that are offered online. One example is Drexel University's graduate-level four-course certificate program in Toxicology and Industrial Hygiene (www.drexel.edu/catalog/certificates/tih.htm). The university recommends that prospective students fill in any gaps they might have in organic chemistry and human physiology by taking these classes at a community college before applying. The four-course program takes one year to complete.

Drexel's program contributes to the "development of expertise particularly in any occupational setting where health and safety concerns are a part of the job.... These courses are also helpful to individuals employed in governmental agencies or businesses involved in the monitoring/regulation of human and environmental exposure to toxic substances." Drexel also offers an online graduate level certificate in Sustainability and Green Construction that provides extensive training in LEED building construction principles.

Readers who have some undergraduate work but want to complete a degree might want to consider the University of Illinois (http://illinois.edu/), which offers a BS-completion program in Environmental Sustainability. There is also a certificate program in Environmental Health Informatics.

The University of Illinois also offers an online certificate in non-profit management. If you are interested in working for a green nonprofit organization, this type of program is an excellent way to prepare, particularly if you can combine this online program with some volunteer experience. The certificate consists of six courses ranging from financial accounting to fundraising management to operations management.

For readers who already have an engineering degree but really want to transition to a green engineering position, the University of Illinois' online Environmental and Water Resources Engineering certificate program could be a way of picking up the needed environmental training without having to leave a job to go back to school. The certificate program consists of seven classes, all offered online.

Bismarck State recently started a Renewable Energy program that is available online as well as on campus (http://info.bismarckstate.edu/energy/). The program offers coursework in power generation and wind energy as well as biomass, hydro, wind, solar, tidal, geothermal, and fuel cell generation of electricity.

Minnesota West Community and Technical College (www.mnwet.edu) offers online certificate programs in both Biofuels Technology—Diesel and Biofuels Technology–Ethanol. Let's say you are interested in the Diesel certificate. The 17-unit certificate program can be taken online and consists of the nine courses ranging from biodiesel technologies to industrial water treatment.

Finally, Boston Architectural College (www.the-bac.edu) offers four different Sustainable Design certificate programs online. These programs were developed in partnership with Building Green, a green building industry organization. The following certificates are offered:

- Sustainable Design
- Sustainable Community Planning and Design
- Sustainable Building Design and Construction
- Sustainable Residential Design

Students must complete six courses to earn a certificate, and the school offers more than thirty different classes to choose from, giving you the flexibility to focus your education to meet your career goals.

Boot Camps

A number of environmental certificates are available after only five or six days of intense work via "boot camps." One prime example is Boots on the Roof (www.bootsontheroof.com). This company offers programs in California and in New Jersey as well as online. Among the boot camp programs are the following:

- Solar PV (6 days)
- Wind Energy (5 days)
- Solar PV for Sales Professionals (4 days)
- Solar Thermal (6 days)

The Solar PV and Wind Energy courses (and certificates) are available online. There also is a Master Certificate in Renewable Energy available that includes Solar, Thermal, Wind, Home Energy Retrofit (BPI/HERZ), and Commercial Solar courses. Although they may not carry the same prestige as a four-year degree, the certificates offered through these boot camps may be the only credential you need to supplement your experience and break into your new green career.

PRACTICING WHAT THEY PREACH

Institutions that not only offer certificates in green occupational areas but also engage in ecofriendly practices are likely to be honest brokers that provide good value because they have made a commitment to be green. One prime example is Red Rocks Community College (www.rrcc.edu) located in Lakewood, Colorado, near Denver. The school has partnered with the National Science Foundation, the Colorado School of Mines, the National Renewable Energy Laboratory, and Jefferson County Schools in an effort to create and sustain a green workforce. Besides offering free green lesson plans to any teacher who is interested and installing its own solar panels, the school offers an incredible number of certificate programs:

- Energy and Industrial Maintenance

- Energy Audit

- Energy Operations and Process Technology

- Environmental Technology

- Renewable Energy

- Water Quality Management

Becoming a Green Activist or Advocate

One green occupation that will always need new people is that of green activist or advocate. Virtually every green organization has room for people at the local level to move politicians and citizens to action. Where do you get training for this type of career? One option is certainly the green organizations themselves. Many offer internal training for members interested in community activism.

Another choice if you're a college graduate is the Green Corps. The Green Corps is a year-long paid training program. This program includes a wide range of experiences and the opportunity to work on environmental issues across the country. The Green Corps sends organizers to jumpstart campaigns for groups such as the Rainforest Action Network, Sierra Club, Greenpeace, and Environment America. People accepted to this program earn a salary of $23,750, but the experience and the skills learned are twice as valuable. You can learn more at www.greencorps.org.

199

Choose Your Program Wisely

Green training is a brand-new field. As such, there are scam artists who have begun selling training programs to capitalize on the popularity of environmental coursework. Unfortunately, assessing a training program's quality from the outside is often difficult.

A number of for-profit schools are beginning to offer various green training programs that include certificates. These programs are far more expensive than programs offered by nonprofit organizations and community colleges. Be sure to investigate the programs you find interesting. Here are some ways to avoid wasting your money and time:

- Ask whether any of the certificates are nationally recognized by well-known green organizations.

- Ask for student references.

- Check online to see whether there are complaints about the programs.

- Compare the content of a certificate program offered by a for-profit institution with similar certificate programs offered by community colleges and universities.

- Check with the HR department of companies that hire in the particular field you're planning to study and see whether the program is recognized or would be valued by the company.

Additional Training Opportunities

We have diligently searched for green training programs of relatively short duration, but it is impossible to include all of them. New training programs are springing up every day. The schools and organizations listed here likely will have even more programs available by the time this book is published. So, if you don't see the exact program that fits your bill, go to the websites of the schools located near you or the national programs and do some digging around. You're bound to find the perfect fit.

Table 10.1 provides a list of training programs, the schools offering these programs, and the state where training takes place. Use it to contact the schools whose programs interest you.

Happy hunting!

Table 10.1: Training Opportunities by Program

Training	State	Institution	Website
Advanced PV Installation	Colorado	Red Rocks Community College	www.rrcc.edu
Advanced Technology Vehicles	Michigan	Lansing Community College	www.lcc.edu
Advanced Wind Energy	Illinois	Sauk Valley Community College	www.svcc.edu
Air Conditioning & Heat Pump	National	Building Performance Institute	www.bpi.org
Air Quality Engineering	Texas	Southern Methodist University	www.smu.edu
Alternative & Sustainable Energy	Nevada	Luna Community College	www.luna.edu
Alternative Energy	Kansas	Colby Community College	www.colbycc.edu
Alternative Energy	Missouri	Crowder College	www.crowder.edu
Alternative Energy & Fuel Cells	Ohio	Hocking College	www.hocking.edu
Alternative Energy Engineering Technology	Michigan	Lansing Community College	www.lcc.edu
Alternative Energy Systems	Virginia	New River Community College	www2.nr.edu
Alternative Energy Systems Technology	Connecticut	Naugatuck Community College	www.nvcc.commnet.edu
Alternative Energy Technology	Arizona	Coconino Community College	www.coconino.edu
Alternative Energy Technology	Michigan	Lansing College	www.lcc.edu
Alternative Energy/ Wind Turbine Technology	Michigan	Delta College	www.delta.edu
Alternative Fuels	New York	Hudson Valley Community College	www.hvcc.edu
Atmospheric Science	Arizona	Arizona State University	www.asu.edu
Atmospheric Sciences	Georgia	University of Georgia	www.uga.edu
Automotive Clean Air Car, Emissions	California	Cerritos Community College	www.cerritos.edu
Automotive Clean Air Car, Emissions	California	College of the Desert	www.collegeofthedesert.edu
Automotive Clean Air Car, Emissions	California	Cypress College	www.cypresscollege.edu
Automotive Clean Air Car, Emissions	California	Fresno City College	www.fresnocitycollege.edu

(continued)

(continued)

Table 10.1: Training Opportunities by Program

Training	State	Institution	Website
Automotive Clean Air Car, Emissions	California	Long Beach City College	www.lbcc.edu
Automotive Clean Air Car, Emissions	California	Rio Hondo Community College	www.riohondo.edu
Automotive Clean Air Car, Emissions	California	San Diego Miramar College	www.sdmiramar.edu
Basic Wind Energy	Illinois	Sauk Valley Community College	www.svcc.edu
Biofuels	North Carolina	Central Carolina Community College	www.cccc.edu
Biofuels Technology	Minnesota	Minnesota West Community and Technical College	www.mnwest.edu
Biomass Operations Technology	Iowa	Des Moines Area Community College	www.dmacc.edu
Biorefinery Technician	Wisconsin	Mid-State Technical College	www.mstc.edu
Biorenewable Fuels Technology	Iowa	Iowa Lakes Community College	www.iowalakes.edu
Building Analyst	National	Building Performance Institute	www.bpi.org
Building Energy Technologies	Illinois	Wilbur Wright College	www.wrightcc.edu
Carbon Reduction Manager	National	Everblue Training Institute	www.everblue.edu
Civil & Environmental Engineering	Massachusetts	Tufts University	www.tufts.edu
Climate Control Technology	Tennessee	Cleveland Community College	www.clevelandstatecc.edu
Coastal Zone Management	Massachusetts	Cape Cod Community College	www.capecod.edu
Community Environmental Studies	Massachusetts	Tufts University	www.tufts.edu
Community Forestry	Georgia	University of Georgia	www.uga.edu
Corporate Sustainability Manager	National	Everblue Training Institute	www.everblue.edu
Decision Making for Climate Change	Online	University of Washington	www.washington.edu
EcoBroker	Online	EcoBroker	www.ecobroker.com
Electric Hybrid & Hydrogen Fuel Cells	California	Cerritos Community College	www.cerritos.edu

Table 10.1: Training Opportunities by Program

Training	State	Institution	Website
Electric Hybrid & Hydrogen Fuel Cells	California	City College of San Francisco	www.ccsf.edu
Electric Hybrid & Hydrogen Fuel Cells	California	College of the Desert	www.collegeofthedesert.edu
Electric Hybrid & Hydrogen Fuel Cells	California	Cypress College	www.cypresscollege.edu
Electric Hybrid & Hydrogen Fuel Cells	California	Fresno City College	www.fresnocitycollege.edu
Electric Hybrid & Hydrogen Fuel Cells	California	Long Beach City College	www.lbcc.edu
Electric Hybrid & Hydrogen Fuel Cells	California	Rio Hondo Community College	www.riohondo.edu
Electric Hybrid & Hydrogen Fuel Cells	California	San Diego Miramar College	www.sdmiramar.edu
Electric Utility Substation Technology	Minnesota	Minnesota West Community and Technical College	www.mnwest.edu
Energy and Resource Management	Oregon	Clackamas Community College	www.clackamas.cc.or.us
Energy and Sustainability	Massachusetts	Tufts University	www.tufts.edu
Energy Audit	National	Green Business Institute	www.buildagreenbusiness.com
Energy Auditor	Massachusetts	Heatspring Learning Institute	www.heatspring.com
Energy Auditor	National	Everblue Training Institute	www.everblue.edu
Energy Efficiency—Energy Auditing	Colorado	Red Rocks Community College	www.rrcc.edu
Energy Efficiency Technician	Michigan	Lansing Community College	www.lcc.edu
Energy Efficiency Technician	Wisconsin	Mid-State Technical College	www.mstc.edu
Energy Management	Massachusetts	Mount Wachusett Community College	www.mwcc.edu
Energy Management	Oregon	Lane Community College	www.lanecc.edu
Energy Management	Washington	Edmonds Community College	www.edcc.edu
Energy Management Technician	Oregon	Lane Community College	www.lanecc.edu
Energy Management Technology	Michigan	Lansing Community College	www.lcc.edu

(continued)

(continued)

Table 10.1: Training Opportunities by Program

Training	State	Institution	Website
Energy Management Technology	Wisconsin	Northeast Wisconsin Technical College	www.nwtc.edu
Energy Performance and Resource Management	Kansas	Johnson County Community College	www.jccc.edu
Energy Technical Specialist	Minnesota	Minnesota West Community and Technical College	www.mnwest.edu
Energy Technology	South Dakota	Lake Area Technical institute	www.lakeareatech.edu
Energy Technology	Texas	Midland College	www.midland.edu
Engineering Geology	Oregon	Portland State University	www.pdx.edu
Entry Level Geothermal Professional	Massachusetts	Heatspring Learning Institute	www.heatspring.com
Envelope	National	Building Performance Institute	www.bpi.org
Environmental and Water Resources Engineering	Massachusetts	Tufts University	www.tufts.edu
Environmental Compliance Operations	Colorado	Red Rocks Community College	www.rrcc.edu
Environmental Control Technology	California	Laney College	www.laney.peralta.edu
Environmental Ethics	Georgia	University of Georgia	www.uga.edu
Environmental Geology	Oregon	Portland State University	www.pdx.edu
Environmental Health and Safety Auditor	Online	Board of Environmental Health and Safety Auditor Certifications	www.beac.org
Environmental Health and Safety Technology	Ohio	Cuyahoga Community College	www.tri-c.edu
Environmental Health Informatics	Online	University of Illinois Global Campus	www.uiuc.edu
Environmental Health Technology	Missouri	Crowder College	www.crowder.edu
Environmental Management	Massachusetts	Tufts University	www.tufts.edu
Environmental Management and Compliance	Texas	Southern Methodist University	www.smu.edu
Environmental Policy (Postbaccalaureate)	Online	University of Massachusetts, Amherst	www.umassonline.net

Table 10.1: Training Opportunities by Program

Training	State	Institution	Website
Environmental Pre-engineering	Colorado	Red Rocks Community College	www.rrcc.edu
Environmental Resources/Energy Management	Florida	St. Petersburg College	www.spcollege.edu
Environmental Restoration	Massachusetts	Tufts University	www.tufts.edu
Environmental Safety Systems	Colorado	Red Rocks Community College	www.rrcc.edu
Environmental Science	Washington	Edmonds Community College	www.edcc.edu
Environmental Science Technology	Florida	St. Petersburg College	www.spcollege.edu
Environmental Science Technology	North Carolina	Wake Technical College	www.waketech.edu
Environmental Studies	Iowa	Iowa Lakes Community College	www.iowalakes.edu
Environmental Systems Engineering	Massachusetts	Tufts University	www.tufts.edu
Environmental Systems in Emerging Technologies	Wisconsin	Fox Valley Technical College	www.fvtc.edu
Environmental Systems Technology	Michigan	Oakland Community College	www.oaklandcc.edu
Environmental Technologies and Sustainable Practices	Washington	Cascadia Community College	www.cascadia.edu
Environmental Technology	Massachusetts	Cape Cod Community College	www.capecod.edu
Environmental Technology	New Mexico	Santa Fe Community College	www.sfccnm.edu
Fisheries Management	Oregon	Oregon State University	www.oregonstate.edu
Fisheries Technology	Alaska	University of Alaska, Fairbanks	www.uaf.edu
Fuel Cell Technology	Ohio	Stark State College of Technology	www.starkstate.edu
Fuel Cell Technology	Texas	Texas State Technical College, Waco	www.waco.tstc.edu
Gaseous Fuels	California	Cerritos Community College	www.cerritos.edu
Gaseous Fuels	California	City College of San Francisco	www.ccsf.edu

(continued)

(continued)

Table 10.1: Training Opportunities by Program

Training	State	Institution	Website
Gaseous Fuels	California	College of the Desert	www.collegeofthedesert.edu
Gaseous Fuels	California	Cypress College	www.cypresscollege.edu
Gaseous Fuels	California	Fresno City College	www.fresnocitycollege.edu
Gaseous Fuels	California	Long Beach City College	www.lbcc.edu
Gaseous Fuels	California	Mission Community College	www.missioncollege.org
Gaseous Fuels	California	Rio Hondo Community College	www.riohondo.edu
Gaseous Fuels	California	San Diego Miramar College	www.sdmiramar.edu
Geographic Information Systems	Georgia	University of Georgia	www.uga.edu
Geographic Information Systems	Massachusetts	Cape Cod Community College	www.capecod.edu
Geographic Information Systems	Michigan	Lansing Community College	www.lcc.edu
Geographic Information Systems	Oregon	Portland State University	www.pdx.edu
Geospatial Science	New Jersey	Rutgers University	www.rutgers.edu
Geotechnical and Geo-environmental Engineering	Massachusetts	Tufts University	www.tufts.edu
Geothermal Technician	Michigan	Lansing Community College	www.lcc.edu
Green Building Systems	New Mexico	Santa Fe Community College	www.sfccnm.edu
Green Business Consultant	Online	Green Business League	www.greencleanconsultant.com
Green Certified Building Inspector	Online	Green Real Estate Education	www.greenrealestateeducation.com
Green Certified Mortgage Professional	Online	Green Real Estate Education	www.greenrealestateeducation.com
Green Certified Real Estate Professional	Online	Green Real Estate Education	www.greenrealestateeducation.com
Green Design	Virginia	Tidewater Community College	www.tcc.edu
Greenhouse Gas Accounting	Online	GHG Management Institute	www.ghginstitute.org
Grid Tie, Entry Level	Colorado	Red Rocks Community College	www.rrcc.edu
Hazardous and Waste Materials Management	Texas	Southern Methodist University	www.smu.edu

Table 10.1: Training Opportunities by Program

Training	State	Institution	Website
Heating	National	Building Performance Institute	www.bpi.org
High Latitude Range Management	Alaska	University of Alaska, Fairbanks	www.uaf.edu
Home Energy Retrofit	National	Green Business Institute	www.buildagreenbusiness.com
Human Dimensions of Environmental Change	New Jersey	Rutgers University	www.humanecology.rutgers.edu
Humanitarian Engineering	Massachusetts	Tufts University	www.tufts.edu
Hybrid Electric Vehicle	Michigan	Macomb Community College	www.macomb.edu
Hydrogeology	Oregon	Portland State University	www.pdx.edu
IGSHPA Geothermal Installer's Course	National	Green Business Institute	www.buildagreenbusiness.com
Industrial Ecology	Michigan	University of Michigan	www.umich.edu
Introduction to Air Compliance	Colorado	Red Rocks Community College	www.rrcc.edu
Introduction to Soil Compliance	Colorado	Red Rocks Community College	www.rrcc.edu
Introduction to Water Compliance	Colorado	Red Rocks Community College	www.rrcc.edu
Introduction to Wind Energy Technology	Colorado	Red Rocks Community College	www.rrcc.edu
Land and Turfgrass Technician	Iowa	Iowa Lakes Community College	www.iowalakes.edu
LEED Green Associate	National	Everblue Training Institute	www.everblue.edu
LEED Green Associate	Online	Green Building Credential Institute	www.gbci.org
Low-Voltage Technician	Colorado	Red Rocks Community College	www.rrcc.edu
Manufactured Housing	National	Building Performance Institute	www.bpi.org
Multifamily Buildings	National	Building Performance Institute	www.bpi.org
Natural Resources Technician	Wisconsin	Fox Valley Technical College	www.fvtc.edu
Occupational Health and Industrial Hygiene	Texas	Southern Methodist University	www.smu.edu
Occupational Safety and Health	Washington	Edmonds Community College	www.edcc.edu

(continued)

(continued)

Table 10.1: Training Opportunities by Program

Training	State	Institution	Website
Photovoltaic Technology	Massachusetts	Cape Cod Community College	www.capecod.edu
Pollution Control and Prevention	Texas	Southern Methodist University	www.smu.edu
Powerline Technology	Minnesota	Minnesota West Community and Technical College	www.mnwest.edu
The Practice & Policy of Composting, Recycling and Waste Prevention	Online	University of Washington	www.washington.edu
Precision Agriculture	Michigan	Lansing Community College	www.lcc.edu
Public Health	Online	University of Washington	www.washington.edu
PV Installation	New York	Hudson Valley Community College	www.hvcc.edu
Renewable Electricity Technician	Wisconsin	Mid-State Technical College	www.mstc.edu
Renewable Energy	New Mexico	San Juan College	www.sanjuancollege.edu
Renewable Energy	Wisconsin	Madison Area Technical College	http://matcmadison.edu
Renewable Energy/ Energy Efficiency	Massachusetts	Greenfield Community College	www.gcc.mass.edu
Renewable Energy for Educators	National	Solar Energy Institute	www.solarenergy.org
Renewable Energy Generation Technology	North Dakota	Bismarck State College	www.bismarckstate.edu
Renewable Energy (Master Certificate)	California	Boots on the Roof	www.bootsontheroof.com
Renewable Energy Specialist	Wisconsin	Mid-State Technical College	www.mstc.edu
Renewable Energy Systems	Iowa	Clinton Community College	www.eicc.edu
Renewable Energy Systems	Iowa	Muscatine Community College	www.eicc.edu
Renewable Energy Systems	Iowa	Scott Community College	www.eicc.edu
Renewable Energy Systems	Oregon	Portland State University	www.pdx.edu
Renewable Energy Technician	Illinois	Kankakee Community College	www.kcc.edu
Renewable Energy Technician	Oregon	Lane Community College	www.lanecc.edu

Table 10.1: Training Opportunities by Program

Training	State	Institution	Website
Renewable Energy Technologies	Pennsylvania	Pennsylvania College of Technology	www.pct.edu
Renewable Energy Technology	Iowa	Indian Hills Community College	www.ihcc.cc.ia.us
Renewable Energy Technology	Oregon	Columbia Gorge Community College	www.cgcc.cc.or.us
Renewable Energy Technology	Oregon	Lane Community College	www.lanecc.edu
Renewable Energy— Wind Technology	Texas	Amarillo College	www.actx.edu
Renewable Thermal Technician	Wisconsin	Mid-State Technical College	www.mstc.edu
Residential Building Envelope Accessible Areas Air Leakage Control Installer	National	Building Performance Institute	www.bpi.org
Residential Building Envelope Whole House Air Leakage Control Chief	National	Building Performance Institute	www.bpi.org
Restoration Horticulture	Washington	Edmonds Community College	www.edcc.edu
Safety, Health and Environmental Awareness	Alaska	University of Alaska, Fairbanks	www.uaf.edu
Science, Technology, and Environmental Policy	New Jersey	Princeton University	www.princeton.edu
Site Assessment	Massachusetts	Cape Code Community College	www.capecod.edu
Small Wind Technology	Massachusetts	Cape Cod Community College	www.capecod.edu
Solar Electric PV Installer	Massachusetts	Heatspring Learning Institute	www.heatspring.com
Solar Electricity (Photovoltaics)	National	Solar Energy Institute	www.solarenergy.org
Solar Energy	New Mexico	Santa Fe Community College	www.sfccnm.edu
Solar Energy Technician	Michigan	Lansing Community College	www.lcc.edu
Solar Energy Technology	Wisconsin	Northeast Wisconsin Technical College	www.nwtc.edu

(continued)

(continued)

Table 10.1: Training Opportunities by Program

Training	State	Institution	Website
Solar Installation	National	North American Board of Certified Energy Practitioners	www.nabcep.org
Solar PV	California	Boots on the Roof	www.bootsontheroof.com
Solar PV	National	Green Business Institute	www.buildagreenbusiness.com
Solar PV Designer	Colorado	Red Rocks Community College	www.rrcc.edu
Solar PV for Sales Professionals	California	Boots on the Roof	www.bootsontheroof.com
Solar Technology	California	Cerro Coso Community College	www.cerrocoso.edu
Solar Technology	Texas	Texas State Technical College, Waco	www.waco.tstc.edu
Solar Thermal	California	Boots on the Roof	www.bootsontheroof.com
Solar Thermal	National	Green Business Institute	www.buildagreenbusiness.com
Solar Thermal	National	Solar Energy Institute	www.solarenergy.org
Solar Thermal Designer	Colorado	Red Rocks Community College	www.rrcc.edu
Solar Thermal (Entry Level)	Colorado	Red Rocks Community College	www.rrcc.edu
Solar Thermal Installer	Colorado	Red Rocks Community College	www.rrcc.edu
Solar Thermal Installer	Massachusetts	Heatspring Learning Institute	www.heatspring.com
Solar Thermal Technology	Massachusetts	Cape Cod Community College	www.capecod.edu
Solar Voltaic Installer	Minnesota	Hibbing Community College	www.hibbing.edu
Solar Voltaic Installer	Wisconsin	Fox Valley Technical College	www.fvtc.edu
Solar Voltaic Manufacturing Technology	Oregon	Portland State University	www.pdx.edu
Solid Waste Management Technology	California	Los Angeles Trade Technical College	www.lattc.edu
Supply Water Technology	California	Los Angeles Trade Technical College	www.lattc.edu
Sustainability	Florida	St. Petersburg College	www.spcollege.edu

Table 10.1: Training Opportunities by Program

Training	State	Institution	Website
Sustainability	Michigan	Lansing Community College	www.lcc.edu
Sustainability	Oregon	Portland State University	www.pdx.edu
Sustainability	Texas	Southern Methodist University	www.smu.edu
Sustainability Studies	Online	University of Massachusetts, Amherst	www.umassonline.edu
Sustainable Agriculture	North Carolina	Central Carolina Community College	www.cccc.edu
Sustainable Building	National	Solar Energy Institute	www.solarenergy.org
Sustainable Construction Technology	Hawaii	Mani Community College	www.maui.hawaii.edu
Sustainable Design	Online	Boston Architectural College	www.the-bac.edu
Sustainable Energy	Indiana	Ivy Tech Community College	www.ivytech.edu
Sustainable Energy Resource Management	Iowa	Iowa Lakes Community College	www.iowalakes.edu
Sustainable Energy Technology	New Jersey	Salem Community College	www.salemcc.edu
Sustainable Green Building	Arizona	Coconino Community College	www.coconino.edu
Sustainable Natural Resources	Oregon	Oregon State University	www.oregonstate.edu
Sustainable Transportation	Online	University of Washington	www.washington.edu
Toxicology and Industrial Hygiene	Online	Drexel University	www.drexel.edu
Transportation	Oregon	Portland State University	www.pdx.edu
Transportation Studies	New Jersey	Rutgers University	www.rutgers.edu
Transportation Systems	Arizona	Arizona State University	www.asu.edu
Transportation Systems	Oregon	Portland State University	www.pdx.edu
Urban Design	Oregon	Portland State University	www.pdx.edu
Urban Landscape and Garden Development	Online	University of Massachusetts, Amherst	www.umassonline.net
Wastewater Management	Massachusetts	Cape Cod Community College	www.capecod.edu

(continued)

(continued)

Table 10.1: Training Opportunities by Program

Training	State	Institution	Website
Wastewater Technology	California	Los Angeles Trade Technical College	www.lattc.edu
Water Conflict Management	Oregon	Oregon State University	www.oregonstate.edu
Water Conservation	New Mexico	Santa Fe Community College	www.sfccnm.edu
Water Conservation Technician	Oregon	Lane Community College	www.lanecc.edu
Water Quality Engineering	Texas	Southern Methodist University	www.smu.edu
Water Resources	Georgia	University of Georgia	www.uga.edu
Water Supply	Massachusetts	Cape Cod Community College	www.capecod.edu
Water Systems, Science and Society	Massachusetts	Tufts University	www.tufts.edu
Wind Energy	California	Boots on the Roof	www.bootsontheroof.com
Wind Energy	Oklahoma	Oklahoma City Community College	www.occc.edu
Wind Energy	Texas	Texas State Technical College, West Texas	www.westtexas.tstc.edu
Wind Energy, Advanced Electrical	Colorado	Red Rocks Community College	www.rrcc.edu
Wind Energy, Advanced Mechanical	Colorado	Red Rocks Community College	www.rrcc.edu
Wind Energy and Turbine Technology	Iowa	Iowa Lakes Community College	www.iowalakes.edu
Wind Energy and Turbine Technology	New York	Clinton Community College	www.clinton.edu
Wind Energy, Basic Electro-Mechanical	Colorado	Red Rocks Community College	www.rrcc.edu
Wind Energy Safety	Colorado	Red Rocks Community College	www.rrcc.edu
Wind Energy Technician	Idaho	College of Southern Idaho	www.csi.edu
Wind Energy Technology	Kansas	Cloud County Community College	www.cloud.edu
Wind Energy Technology	Michigan	Kalamazoo Valley Community College	www.kvcc.edu
Wind Energy Technology	Minnesota	Minnesota West Community and Technical College	www.mnwest.edu

Table 10.1: Training Opportunities by Program

Training	State	Institution	Website
Wind Energy Technology	New Mexico	Mesalands Community College	www.mesalands.edu
Wind Energy Technology	Wisconsin	Lakeshore Technical College	http://gotoltc.edu
Wind Energy Technology	Wyoming	Laramie County Community College	www.lccc.wy.edu
Wind Power	National	Green Business Institute	www.buildagreenbusiness.com
Wind Power	National	Solar Energy Institute	www.solarenergy.org
Wind Power Technology	Maine	Northern Maine Community College	www.nmcc.edu
Wind Technician	New York	Hudson Valley Community College	www.hvcc.edu
Wind Technology	California	Cerro Coso Community College	www.cerrocoso.edu
Wind Turbine Technician	Illinois	Highland Community College	www.highland.edu
Wind Turbine Technician	Michigan	Lansing Community College	www.lcc.edu
Wind Turbine Technician	Online	Pinnacle Career Institute	www.pcitraining.edu
Wind Turbine Technology	Iowa	Des Moines Area Community College	www.dmacc.edu
Wind Turbine Technology	Ohio	Lorain County Community College	www.lorainccc.edu
Wind Turbine Technology	South Dakota	Mitchell Technical Institute	www.mitchelltech.edu
Zero Energy Housing	Tennessee	Cleveland State Community College	www.clevelandstatecc.edu

CHAPTER 11

Resources for Green Career Changers

In this chapter, we have assembled a list of major volunteer and professional organizations, including the Web address of these groups as well as a brief description. There are hundreds of such organizations, so this list is far from complete. We have not included some major groups such as the Environmental Defense Fund and Friends of the Earth that focus on donations rather than active participation. Please note that we have included the organizations' own descriptions found on their websites whenever possible.

Volunteer Organizations

ActivistsWanted.org
www.activistswanted.org
The mission of ActivistsWanted.org is to motivate and empower caring people like you to participate in action that will reverse global destruction. We encourage you to join us and become informed and involved. We must stand together to hold corporations and the government accountable for the destruction. Help us bring about the changes that will save our Earth.

The Clean Water Network
www.cleanwater.org
The Clean Water Network (CWN) is a national coalition of more than 1,200 local, state, and national non-profit public interest organizations working together to protect the health, safety, and quality of our nation's waters. It is the largest advocacy coalition in the country working to protect our nation's water resources.

Defenders of Wildlife
www.defenders.org
Founded in 1947, Defenders of Wildlife is one of the country's leaders in science-based, results-oriented wildlife conservation. We stand out in our commitment to saving imperiled wildlife and championing the Endangered Species Act, the landmark law that protects them.

Earth First!
www.earthfirstjournal.org
Earth First! formed in 1979, in response to an increasingly corporate, compromising and ineffective environmental community. It is not an organization, but a movement. There are no "members" of EF!, only Earth First!ers. We believe in using all of the tools in the toolbox, from

grassroots and legal organizing to civil disobedience and monkey wrenching. When the law won't fix the problem, we put our bodies on the line to stop the destruction. Earth First!'s direct-action approach draws attention to the crises facing the natural world, and it saves lives.

Earth Island Institute
www.earthisland.org
Earth Island Institute is a non-profit, public interest, membership organization that supports people who are creating solutions to protect our shared planet.

Greenpeace
www.greenpeace.org
Greenpeace is the leading independent campaigning organization that uses peaceful direct action and creative communication to expose global environmental problems and to promote solutions that are essential to a green and peaceful future.

The Groundwater Foundation
www.groundwater.org
The Groundwater Foundation is a nonprofit organization that educates people and inspires action to ensure sustainable, clean groundwater for future generations.

International Association for Environmental Hydrology
www.hydroweb.com
The International Association for Environmental Hydrology is a worldwide association for hydrology and the environment, dedicated to cleanup of fresh water resources. IAEH publishes the Journal of Environmental Hydrology, Hydrology News, and the HydroKit series of hydrology software modeling packages.

National Audubon Society
www.audubon.org
Audubon's Mission: To conserve and restore natural ecosystems, focusing on birds, other wildlife, and their habitats for the benefit of humanity and the earth's biological diversity.

National Campaign for Sustainable Agriculture
www.sustainableculture.net
The National Sustainable Agriculture Coalition (NSAC) is an alliance of grassroots organizations that advocates for federal policy reform to advance the sustainability of agriculture, food systems, natural resources, and rural communities.

The National Coalition for Marine Conservation
www.savethefish.org
Founded in 1973, the National Coalition for Marine Conservation (NCMC) is the USA's oldest public advocacy group dedicated exclusively to conserving ocean fish, such as swordfish, marlin, sharks, tuna, striped bass, menhaden and herring.

National Wildlife Federation
www.nwf.org
The National Wildlife Federation is America's largest conservation organization. We work with more than 4 million members, partners and supporters in communities across the country to protect and restore wildlife habitat, confront global warming and connect with nature.

The Nature Conservancy
www.nature.org
The Nature Conservancy is the leading conservation organization working around the world to protect ecologically important lands and waters for nature and people.

Oceana
http://na.oceana.org
Oceana, founded in 2001, is the largest international organization focused solely on ocean conservation. Our offices in North America, Central America, South

America and Europe work together on a limited number of strategic, directed campaigns to achieve measurable outcomes that will help return our oceans to former levels of abundance.

One Earth One Mission

www.oeom.org

As a synergistically designed platform for the environment, animal rights, health, and other issues, OEOM will inform, enlighten, and actively engage all citizens concerned about the future of Earth.

Rainforest Action Network

www.ran.org

Rainforest Action Network (RAN) is headquartered in San Francisco, California, with offices staff in Tokyo, Japan, and Edmonton, Canada, plus thousands of volunteer scientists, teachers, parents, students and other concerned citizens around the world. We believe that a sustainable world can be created in our lifetime, and that aggressive action must be taken immediately to leave a safe and secure world for our children.

The Rainforest Alliance

www.rainforest-alliance.org

The Rainforest Alliance works to conserve biodiversity and ensure sustainable livelihoods by transforming land-use practices, business practices and consumer behavior.

The Sierra Club

www.sierraclub.org

Since 1892, the Sierra Club has been working to protect communities, wild places, and the planet itself. We are the oldest, largest, and most influential grassroots environmental organization in the United States. And our founder, John Muir, appears on the back of the California quarter.

Soil and Water Conservation Society

www.swcs.org

Soil and Water Conservation Society (SWCS) is a nonprofit scientific and educational organization—founded in 1943—that serves as an advocate for conservation professionals and for science-based conservation practice, programs, and policy. SWCS has over 5,000 members around the world. They include researchers, administrators, planners, policymakers, technical advisors, teachers, students, farmers, and ranchers. Our members come from nearly every academic discipline and many different public, private, and nonprofit institutions.

TreePeople

www.treepeople.org

TreePeople's mission is to inspire, engage, and support people to take personal responsibility for the urban environment, making it safe, healthy, fun, and sustainable and to share the process as a model for the world.

Water Environment Federation

www.wef.org

The Water Environment Federation is a not-for-profit association that provides technical education and training for thousands of water quality professionals who clean water and return it safely to the environment. WEF members have proudly protected public health, served their local communities, and supported clean water worldwide since 1928.

The Wildlife Society

http://joomla.wildlife.org/

Members manage, conserve, and study wildlife populations and habitats. They actively manage forests, conserve wetlands, restore endangered species, conserve wildlife on private and public lands, resolve wildlife damage and disease problems, and enhance biological diversity.

Professional Associations

Air and Waste Management Association
www.awma.org

The Air & Waste Management Association (A&WMA) is a nonprofit, nonpartisan professional organization that enhances knowledge and expertise by providing a neutral forum for information exchange, professional development, networking opportunities, public education, and outreach to more than 8,000 environmental professionals in 65 countries. A&WMA also promotes global environmental responsibility and increases the effectiveness of organizations to make critical decisions that benefit society.

Algal Biomass Association
www.algalbiomass.org

The Algal Biomass Organization promotes the development of viable technologies and commercial markets for renewable and sustainable products derived from algae.

Alliance for Sustainable Built Environments
www.greenerfacilities.org

In 2003, an exclusive group of international building industry manufacturers with a similar approach to business banded together and committed to an aggressive, coordinated campaign to inform decision-makers that the choices they make with regard to their facilities can be economically and environmentally sustainable. The consortium was named the Alliance for Sustainable Built Environments (ASBE).

Alliance of Certified Hazardous Materials Managers
www.achmm.org

The Alliance of Hazardous Materials Professionals™ (AHMP), formerly the Academy of Certified Hazardous Materials Managers, Inc. (ACHMM) is a professional association with a membership of more than 4,000 of the nation's leading experts in environmental, health, safety and security management. AHMP is the only national organization devoted to the professional advancement of the hazardous materials management field.

American Academy of Environmental Engineers
www.aaee.net

The American Academy of Environmental Engineers is dedicated to excellence in the practice of environmental engineering to ensure the public health, safety, and welfare to enable humankind to coexist in harmony with nature.

American Council for Energy-Efficient Economy
www.aceee.org

The American Council for an Energy-Efficient Economy is a nonprofit, 501(c)(3) organization dedicated to advancing energy efficiency as a means of promoting economic prosperity, energy security, and environmental protection.

American Fisheries Association
www.fisheries.org

The mission of the American Fisheries Society is to improve the conservation and sustainability of fishery resources and aquatic ecosystems by advancing fisheries and aquatic science and promoting the development of fisheries professionals.

American Geophysical Union

www.agu.org

The American Geophysical Union (AGU), which was established in 1919 by the National Research Council and for more than 50 years operated as an unincorporated affiliate of the National Academy of Sciences, is now a nonprofit corporation chartered under the laws of the District of Columbia. The Union is dedicated to the furtherance of the geophysical sciences through the individual efforts of its members and in cooperation with other national and international scientific organizations.

American Industrial Hygiene Association

www.aiha.org

American Industrial Hygiene Association is one of the largest international associations serving the needs of occupational and environmental health professionals practicing industrial hygiene in industry, government, labor, academic institutions, and independent organizations.

American Institute of Hydrology

www.aihydrology.org

The purpose of AIH is to enhance and strengthen the standing of hydrology as a science and a profession by:

- Establishing standards and procedures to certify individuals qualified in surface-water, groundwater, and water-quality hydrology.
- Establishing and maintaining ethical standards to protect the public from irresponsible work.
- Providing education and training in hydrology.
- Providing the public and government advice and guidance concerning activities related to the hydrologic profession.

The American Society of Heating, Refrigerating and Air-Conditioning Engineers

www.ashrae.org

The American Society of Heating, Refrigerating and Air-Conditioning Engineers advances technology to serve humanity and promote a sustainable world. Membership is open to any person associated with the field.

American Solar Energy Society

www.ases.org

Established in 1954, the nonprofit American Solar Energy Society (ASES) is the nation's leading association of solar professionals and advocates. Our mission is to inspire an era of energy innovation and speed the transition to a sustainable energy economy. We advance education, research, and policy.

American Water Resources Association

www.awra.org

Founded in 1964, the American Water Resources Association is a non-profit professional association dedicated to the advancement of men and women in water resources management, research, and education. AWRA's membership is multidisciplinary; its diversity is its hallmark. It is the professional home of a wide variety of water resources experts including engineers, educators, foresters, biologists, ecologists, geographers, managers, regulators, hydrologists, and attorneys.

American Water Works Association

www.awwa.org

Founded in 1881, American Water Works Association (AWWA) is the authoritative resource on safe water, providing knowledge, information, and advocacy to improve the quality and supply of water in North America and beyond.

AWWA advances public health, safety, and welfare by uniting the efforts of the full spectrum of the water community. AWWA is an international nonprofit and educational society and the largest and oldest organization of water professionals in the world. Its more than 60,000 members represent the full spectrum of the water community: treatment plant operators and managers, scientists, environmentalists, manufacturers, academicians, regulators, and others who hold genuine interest in water supply and public health.

American Wind Energy Association
www.awea.org
AWEA is a national trade association representing wind power project developers, equipment suppliers, services providers, parts manufacturers, utilities, researchers, and others involved in the wind industry—one of the world's fastest-growing energy industries. In addition, AWEA represents hundreds of wind energy advocates from around the world.

Association for the Environmental Health of Soils (AEHS)
www.aehs.com
The Association for Environmental Health and Sciences (AEHS) was created to facilitate communication and foster cooperation among professionals concerned with the challenge of soil protection and cleanup.... AEHS members represent the many disciplines involved in making decisions and solving problems affecting soils, including chemistry, geology, hydrogeology, law, engineering, modeling, toxicology, regulatory science, public health, and public policy.

The Association of Climate Change Officers
www.accoonline.org
The Association of Climate Change Officers (ACCO) is a professional development organization and society that endeavors to:

- Advance the professional knowledge, skills, and experience of those addressing the business and operating implications of climate change in industry, academia, NGOs, and government;

- Provide a forum for the exchange and enhancement of best practices, industry standards, and innovation in the area of climate change strategies;

- Educate industry and government on the importance of employing qualified professionals, developing sound organizational structures, and establishing incentives to encourage innovation; and

- Support members in developing, directing and implementing climate change strategies in their respective organizations.

Association of Conservation Engineers
www.conservationengineers.org
Our members freely share their experience and information pertaining to conservation engineering to make our natural resources more accessible and enjoyable to everyone.

The Association of Consulting Foresters of America
www.acf-foresters.org
The mission of the Association of Consulting Foresters is to promote ethical stewardship of forest resources by advancing the Profession of Consulting Forestry.

Association of Environmental and Engineering Geologists

www.aegweb.org

The Association of Environmental and Engineering Geologists (AEG) contributes to its members' professional success and the public welfare by providing leadership, advocacy, and applied research in environmental and engineering geology.

Association of Environmental Professionals

www.califaep.org

As our name suggests, AEP is a non-profit organization of professionals working to improve our skills as environmental practitioners and natural resource managers. AEP is dedicated to the enhancement, maintenance, and protection of the natural and human environment.

Association of Water Technology

www.awt.org

The Association of Water Technology is a trade group of over 500 companies dedicated to the highest standards of performance in the water treatment industry. We serve member firms by providing business and professional education and resource support, and enable our members' success by facilitating knowledge sharing among members. As the largest association for water treatment specialists, we assist water treatment firms to successfully compete in the industry by promoting activities that enhance a professional and profitable business environment.

Biomass Energy Research Association

www.beraonline.org

An association of bioenergy researchers, companies, and advocates that promotes education and research on renewable biomass energy and waste-to-energy systems.

Biomass Power Association

www.usabiomass.org

The Biomass Power Association is a member-driven, member-focused organization. Our goal is to advance the use of biopower throughout the United States and improve opportunities for each of our unique members. To achieve this, we provide aggressive industry representation at the state and federal level, provide timely briefings to keep our members fully informed about emerging tax and non-tax issues and changing energy policies, and educate policymakers and the public on biopower issues.

Ecological Society of America

www.esa.org

The Ecological Society of America (ESA) is a nonpartisan, nonprofit organization of scientists founded in 1915 to:

- Promote ecological science by improving communication among ecologists;
- Raise the public's level of awareness of the importance of ecological science;
- Increase the resources available for the conduct of ecological science; and ensure the appropriate use of ecological science in environmental decision making by enhancing communication between the ecological community and policy-makers.

Electric Auto Association

www.eaaev.org

The Electric Auto Association (EAA) was formed in 1967 by Walter Laski in San Jose, California. The EAA is a non-profit educational organization that promotes the advancement and widespread adoption of electric vehicles.

Electric Drive Transportation Association
www.electricdrive.org
Founded in 1989, EDTA is the preeminent industry association dedicated to advancing electric drive as a core technology on the road to sustainable mobility. As an advocate for the adoption of electric drive technologies, EDTA serves as the unified voice for the industry and is the primary source of information and education related to electric drive. Our membership includes a diverse representation of vehicle and equipment manufacturers, energy providers, component suppliers, and end users.

Energy and Environmental Building Alliance
www.eeba.org
The Energy & Environmental Building Alliance (EEBA) provides an invaluable platform for insight, collaboration, and education. EEBA delivers unique and relevant, multi-platform educational resources with the intention to manifest sustainable and responsible building principles in the design, marketing, and execution of the building process.

Environmental Bankers Association
www.envirobank.org
Environmental Bankers Association (EBA) is a non-profit trade association that represents the financial services industry, including bank and non-bank financial institutions, insurers, and those who provide services to them. Its members include lending institutions, property & casualty and life insurers, the environmental consulting and appraisal community, and attorneys. The EBA was established in 1994 in response to heightened sensitivity to environmental risk issues, and the need for environmental risk management and due diligence policies and procedures in financial institutions.

Environmental Solutions Association
www.esaassociation.com
Environmental Solutions Association (ESA) is the nation's premier Indoor Air Quality training organization. ESA provides industry professionals with the training and education necessary to confront the environmental and safety issues faced by today's property owners. Our Training and Education courses include Mold Inspection Training, Radon Training for Inspection and Testing, and Indoor Air Quality Training for Inspection and Testing.

Geothermal Energy Association
www.geo-energy.org
The Geothermal Energy Association is a trade association composed of U.S. companies who support the expanded use of geothermal energy and are developing geothermal resources worldwide for electrical power generation and direct-heat uses.

The Indoor Air Quality Association
www.iaqa.org
The Indoor Air Quality Association (IAQA) is a nonprofit, multi-disciplined organization, dedicated to promoting the exchange of indoor environmental information, through education and research, for the safety and well being of the general public.

International Society of Environmental Forensics
www.environmentalforensics.org
The International Society of Environmental Forensics (ISEF) has grown out of the need for a platform to present scientific investigations that address environmental contamination

subjected to law, public debate, or formal argumentation as well as the evaluation of the basic science that serves as underpinnings to those activities. The goal of the ISEF is to regularly provide workshops and training on subject matter encompassing all aspects of contamination within the environmental media of air, water, soil, and biota.

International Society of Sustainability Professionals

http://sustainabilityprofessionals.org
This is a non-profit, member-driven association for professionals who are committed to making sustainability standard practice. Members share resources and best practices, and develop themselves professionally. Special reports, salary surveys, and the upcoming competency study are just a sampling of the rich content offered members.

International Solid Waste Management Association

www.iswa.org
The International Solid Waste Association (ISWA) is an international, independent and non-profit making association, working in the public interest to promote and develop sustainable waste management worldwide. ISWA has members around the world and is the only worldwide association promoting sustainable and professional waste management. The Association is open to individuals and organizations from the scientific community, public institutions, and public and private companies from all over the world working in the field of and interested in waste management.

National Association of Environmental Professionals

www.naep.org
NAEP is...

- the multi-disciplinary association for professionals dedicated to the advancement of the environmental professions.

- a forum for state-of-the-art information on environmental planning, research, and management.

- a network of professional contacts and exchange of information among colleagues in industry, government, academia, and the private sector.

- a resource for structured career development from student memberships to certification as an environmental professional.

- a strong proponent of ethics and the highest standards of practice in the environmental professions.

National Biodiesel Board

www.biodiesel.org
The NBB is the national trade association representing the biodiesel industry as the coordinating body for research and development in the U.S. It was founded in 1992 by state soybean commodity groups, who were funding biodiesel research and development programs. Since that time, the NBB has developed into a comprehensive industry association, which coordinates and interacts with a broad range of cooperators including industry, government, and academia.

National Environmental Health Association

www.neha.org
NEHA will continue to serve you throughout your career as an EH&P professional by fostering cooperation

and understanding between and among environmental health professionals, contributing to the resolution of the worldwide environmental health issues, and by working with other national professional societies to advance the cause, the image, and the professional standing of the environmental health profession. At the same time, NEHA remains solidly founded by its roots in efforts to improve the environment in cities, towns, and rural areas throughout the world in order to create a more healthful environment and quality of life for us all.

National Environmental Training Association
www.neshta.org
NESHTA is a non-profit educational society for environmental, safety, health and other technical training and adult education professionals. Founded in 1977 with assistance and guidance from the U.S. EPA, NESHTA's mission is to promote trainer competency through trainer skills training, continuing education, voluntary certification, peer networking, and the adoption of national and international training and trainer standards.

National Ground Water Association
www.ngwa.org
The National Ground Water Association is the hallmark organization for anyone affiliated with the ground water industry. A nonprofit organization, NGWA is comprised of more than 13,000 U.S. and international ground water professionals—contractors, scientists and engineers, equipment manufacturers, and suppliers. Our purpose is to provide guidance to members, government representatives, and the public for sound scientific, economic, and beneficial development, protection, and management of the world's ground water resources.

National Hydrogen Association
www.hydrogenassociation.org
The National Hydrogen Association is a membership organization founded by a group of ten industry, university, research, and small business members in 1989. Today the NHA's membership has grown to over 100 members, including representatives from the automobile industry; the fuel cell industry; aerospace; federal, state, and local government; energy providers; and many other industry stakeholders. The NHA serves as a catalyst for information exchange and cooperative projects and provides the setting for mutual support among industry, government, and research/academic organizations.

National Hydropower Association
www.hydro.org
The National Hydropower Association (NHA) is a nonprofit national association dedicated exclusively to advancing the interests of the hydropower industry. It seeks to secure hydropower's place as a climate-friendly, renewable, and reliable energy source that serves national environmental and energy policy objectives.

National Onsite Wastewater Recycling Association
www.nowra.org
The National Onsite Wastewater Recycling Association (NOWRA) is the largest organization within the U.S. dedicated solely to educating and representing members within the onsite and decentralized industry. NOWRA headquarters are located in Tacoma, Washington, with constituent local groups throughout the U.S. and Canada.

National Registry of Environmental Professionals

www.nrep.org

We at the NREP are dedicated to professionally and legally enhancing the recognition of those individuals who possess the education, training, and experience as qualified environmental engineers, technologists, managers, technicians, and scientists. We aim to consolidate such recognition into a single, viable source so that the public at large, the government, insurers, and employers can easily see, understand, and justify the importance of these individuals.

National Water Resources Association

www.nwra.org

The National Water Resources Association is a nonprofit federation of state organizations whose membership includes rural water districts, municipal water entities, commercial companies, and individuals. The association is concerned with the appropriate management, conservation, and use of water and land resources on a national scope.

Renewable Fuels Association

www.ethanolrfa.org

As the national trade association for the U.S. ethanol industry, the Renewable Fuels Association (RFA) promotes policies, regulations, and research and development initiatives that will lead to the increased production and use of fuel ethanol. RFA membership includes a broad cross-section of businesses, individuals, and organizations dedicated to the expansion of the U.S. fuel ethanol industry.

Society of Ecological Restoration

http://ser.org/

A non-profit organization infused with the energy of 2,300 members—individuals and organizations who are actively engaged in ecologically sensitive repair and management of ecosystems through an unusually broad array of experience, knowledge sets, and cultural perspectives. They are scientists, planners, administrators, ecological consultants, first peoples, landscape architects, philosophers, teachers, engineers, natural areas managers, writers, growers, community activists, and volunteers, among others.

Society of Environmental Journalists

www.sej.org

The mission of the Society of Environmental Journalists is to strengthen the quality, reach, and viability of journalism across all media to advance public understanding of environmental issues.

Society of Environmental Toxicology and Chemistry

www.setac.org

The Society of Environmental Toxicology and Chemistry (SETAC) is a nonprofit, worldwide professional society comprised of individuals and institutions engaged in:

- the study, analysis, and solution of environmental problems
- the management and regulation of natural resources
- environmental education
- research and development

Solar Energy Industries Association

www.seia.org

Established in 1974, the Solar Energy Industries Association is the national trade association of the solar energy industry. As the voice of the industry, SEIA works to make solar a mainstream and significant energy source by expanding markets, removing market barriers, strengthening the industry, and educating the public on the benefits of solar energy.

Solid Waste Association of North America

www.swana.org

For over 40 years, the Solid Waste Association of North America has been the leading professional association in the solid waste field. Our association serves municipal solid waste professionals throughout North America with conferences, certifications, publications, and technical training courses.

Sustainable Buildings Industry Council

www.sbicouncil.org

The Sustainable Buildings Industry Council (SBIC) is an independent, non-profit organization and a pioneer advocate of the whole building approach to sustainable facilities. We were founded in 1980 as the Passive Solar Industries Council by the major building trade groups, large corporations, small businesses, and individual practitioners who recognized that energy- and resource-efficient design and construction are imperative to a sustainable built environment.

U.S. Green Building Council

www.usgbc.org

The U.S. Green Building Council is a 501(c)(3) non-profit community of leaders working to make green buildings available to everyone within a generation.

Water Quality Association

www.wqa.org

The Water Quality Association (WQA) is a not-for-profit international trade association representing the residential, commercial, industrial, and small community water treatment industry. WQA maintains a close dialogue with other organizations representing different aspects of the water industry in order to best serve consumers, government officials, and industry members.

Windustry

www.windustry.org

Windustry® promotes progressive renewable energy solutions and empowers communities to develop and own wind energy as an environmentally sustainable asset. Through member-supported outreach, education, and advocacy we work to remove the barriers to broad community ownership of wind energy.

Environmental Job Websites

Biodiesel-Jobs.com

www.biodieseljobs.com

Includes resume information, a cost of living calculator for cities, and other city data.

Careers in Wind

www.careersinwind.com

This site, sponsored by the American Wind Energy Association, is a job board that does not require AWEA membership.

Clean Edge

www.cleanedge.com

Offers the "latest news, events, and other resources on clean energy, transportation, water, and materials." The site includes a job board and even a map to examine at a glance where the jobs are located.

Clean Techies

http://cleantechies.com

This site describes itself as "a leading online cleantech destination, green career site & environmental business network on clean technology. It provides insight, orientation, and opportunities for the Clean Tech community." The site includes a job board and a resume writing service.

EcoEmploy

www.ecoemploy.com

Allows searching by state and provides a lengthy list of environmental employers, including federal and state employers.

Eco.org

www.eco.org

Our focus is helping quality job candidates looking for green jobs connect with eco-employers who care about the environment and have green jobs to fill.

Energy Careers

www.energycareers.com

Includes renewable energy as one of its job categories.

Environmental Career Center

www.environmentalcareer.com

The Environmental Career Center is North America's most experienced recruiting and resource firm for the environmental, building, and energy sectors with over 30 years of experience bringing together leading environmental employers with the best candidates for a better environment.

Environmental Career Opportunities

www.ecojobs.com

Subscription to this site's services is fee based. The website states: "Our environmental job vacancies are from all sectors of the job-market including non-profits, corporations, professional firms, institutions, and Federal, state and local government."

Environmental Jobs.com

www.environmentaljobs.com

The following employment opportunity categories are available:

- Environmental Science Jobs
- Advocacy & Policy Jobs
- Renewable Energy Jobs
- Environmental Engineering Jobs
- Health & Safety Jobs
- Environmental Administration & Management Jobs

Ethanol-Jobs.com

www.ethanol-jobs.com

A companion to the diesel-jobs.com website. It also provides city cost of living data and resume information.

Great Green Careers

www.greatgreencareers.com

Published by the same company that publishes *Mother Earth News*. This site "promises to connect employers and job seekers in the green jobs industries," including energy environment, skilled trades, and transportation.

Green Career Central

www.greencareercentral.com

This is a subscription site that charges $49 for three months, though it does offer career coaching.

Green Energy Jobs.com

www.greenenergyjobs.com

Green Energy Jobs offers a global platform for the latest vacancies in the renewable energy sector.

Green Engineering Jobs.com

www.greenengineeringjobs.com

Jobs on this site are categorized as follows: Environment Jobs, Air, Air Quality, Engineering Jobs, Geotechnical Engineer, Structural Engineering, Environmental Engineer, Environmental Engineering,

Civil Engineering Jobs, and Hydraulic Engineering.

Green Job Spider
www.greenjobspider.com
Excellent site that consolidates green job postings from across the Web.

Green Jobs
www.greenjobs.com
Bringing recruiters and job seekers together in the renewable energy sector.

GreenBiz.com
www.greenbiz.com
Find the sustainability professional and green-collar job that's right for you. GreenBiz.com's green jobs and career center has jobs in solar and renewable energy, cleantech, green building, sustainable businesses and socially responsible organizations, and more. Employers can post jobs and internships for free.

NatureJobs.com
www.nature.com/naturejobs/science/
Naturejobs.com is the worldwide career resource for scientists, providing a wide range of career advice and information across Nature Publishing Group journals as well as centrally at naturejobs.com.

Orion Grassroots Network
http://jobs.oriongrassroots.org
This website permits searching by a number of criteria including experience level.

Renewable Energy Jobs
www.renewableenenergyjobs.com
UK-based, this site is trying to build a worldwide database of green jobs. It covers the following categories: Carbon Capture & Storage, Consulting, Energy Efficiency, Geothermal Energy, Hydro Power, Solar Power, Wind Energy, Waste to Energy.

SmartGrid Careers
www.smartgridcareers.com
Besides a comprehensive listing of smart grid jobs, this site also includes a directory of smart grid employers.

Solar Energy Industries Association
www.seia.org
This organization has an extensive job board focused on solar energy jobs.

Stopdodo
www.stopdodo.com
This site lists international environmental jobs and is searchable by category, location, and keyword.

Sustainable Business.com
www.sustainablebusiness.com
This site features what it calls "dream jobs." The site calls itself "Your home for green jobs: renewable and clean energy jobs (solar, wind jobs), green building jobs, organic jobs, and all environmental and sustainable jobs."

SustainLane
www.sustainlane.com
This site describes itself as "an online community where you can connect with local people interested in living healthy lives on a green planet." There is a job board labeled "Green Collar Job Board."

Treehugger.com
www.treehugger.com
Includes a job board with the opportunity to get job alerts via e-mail.

Yahoo! Hot Jobs
http://hotjobs.yahoo.com
Includes a green jobs category as well as articles on green jobs.

INDEX

6833